MARRIAGE:
FOR & AGAINST

MARRIAGE: FOR & AGAINST

INTRODUCTION BY HAROLD H. HART

Hart Publishing Company, Inc.

New York City

Contents

Introduction

ACCORDING TO The New York Times of December 1, 1971, federal statisticians report that marriage as an institution is more popular today than it ever has been in the history of the United States. While in 1890, the first year for which accurate statistics are available, only half of all Americans above fourteen were married, today more than two-thirds of all Americans above that age are married. Furthermore, the incidence of marriage in the general population seems to be increasing. Last year, the rate of weddings per capita was the highest it has been in two decades.

Against this background, it may seem paradoxical that marriage as an institution has never been under more serious attack than it is today. This may, in part, be the result of a fact loudly blazoned in press and in pulpit that today's divorce rate is the highest it has ever been in history.

There has been a plethora of articles in magazines decrying the restrictions of marriage; sociologists increasingly question whether conventional marriage is on the way out; and Women's Libbers are shouting and protesting that marriage merely ossifies unfairness towards the feminine sex.

Over and above this verbal tirade, an appreciable number of people have taken up life styles that are at considerable variance with the concept of marriage as we have known it for centuries. Many of the new communes are structured along lines which scorn our time-honored concepts of the relationship between man and wife; and many people are deliberately experimenting with new relationships which would have been considered so outrageous a decade ago that even notice of such arrangements would have been unlikely to come into the public prints.

One of the striking things about this book is that a large number of well-respected thinkers and sociologists are now considering these new marriage forms so seriously. A number of writers soberly discuss the validity of what sociologists are pleased to term triads, quadrads, etc. Marriage between three people, marriage between two couples, marriage between two people of the same sex, are evaluated, as well as the effect on marriage of the participation of husband and wife in group sex activities. While the consensus seems to be that none of these forms is likely to prove more durable or more satisfying for most people than conventional marriage has been, nevertheless it is refreshing that these new ideas are treated with neither shock nor horror, but with cool detachment and careful analysis. This fact in itself seems to indicate that in our generation we have reached a new level of willingness to examine radical social ideas openly, seriously, critically. Talk of new marriage forms is obviously no longer anathema. This, in and of itself, does not indicate that any of these new forms will prevail and replace marriage; but the new attitude indicates that thinkers, sociologists, doctors, social workers, psychologists, marriage counsellors, etc., understand what has not been quite so clearly understood before: that marriage, like any other human institution, is fallible. Today, the imperfections of marriage are openly acknowledged. Today, there is a striving to experiment in order to achieve betterment. Heretofore, such behavior—and even such attitudes— would have been hopelessly hobbled by religious conviction and by public outrage.

Nevertheless, despite this change in tone, it is interesting to note that most of the writers in this book firmly believe that marriage as a basic relationship between a man and a woman is likely to endure. Most essays indicate, however, that the ground rules are being changed and that they will most likely continue to be changed. What the new ground rules are or should be is the intriguing subject matter of this most provocative discussion.

HAROLD H. HART

MARRIAGE:
FOR & AGAINST

Nathan W. Ackerman was recognized as a foremost authority in the field of family therapy. As Director of the Professional Program of the Family Institute, he trained psychologists and psychiatrists in methods of treating problems between parent and child, and husband and wife.

Dr. Ackerman served as Clinical Professor of Psychiatry at Columbia University, and Visiting Professor at the Albert Einstein College of Medicine. He lectured at universities and hospitals in the United States, and before university medical groups and professional societies throughout the world.

He is the author of FAMILY THERAPY, PSYCHODYNAMICS OF FAMILY LIFE, *and* TREATING THE TROUBLED FAMILY.

Dr. Ackerman completed his contribution to this volume shortly before his death.

Nathan W. Ackerman

ASK ANYONE YOU KNOW "Are you for marriage?"—the likely response is "*Yes, but!*" The *but* stirs a rush of feeling, an endless series of qualifications. It all depends: *A good marriage or a bad one? Your marriage or mine? Marriage as it used to be, or marriage as it is today?* The more honest the confrontation, the more one is flooded with doubt.

One need not seek far for an explanation. The fact is that there is a built-in ambivalence toward the bond of marriage: the flaw is human nature itself. Husband and wife may love one another, or they may loathe one another—but they cannot be indifferent.

The joining of man and woman is a quest for completion. Each seeks in the other wholeness, intimacy, and security. Together, they strive for a sense of immortality through their children. Yet, all the while, they yearn to be free. One struggles ceaselessly for a tolerable balance between commitment to his or her partner and the striving for personal emancipation. On one side lies a dream of fulfillment; on the other, the fear of a yoke or a death trap.

Schopenhauer bequeathed to us a parable about this dilemma: On a bitter winter day, two porcupines moved together to keep warm. Soon they hurt each other with their quills, so they moved apart, only to find themselves freezing again. The poor porcupines moved back and forth, freezing and hurting, until they finally found the optimum distance at which they could huddle in warmth, and yet not pain each other too much. Have husbands and wives yet discovered that optimum distance?

Marriage has three main aspects: the bond of love and sex, mutual aid in the struggle for existence, and the desire for children. Its irreducible minimum is the triad of mother, father, and child. Children bind the couple as parents, but less so sexually. By its very nature, the sex act is come and go; surely it doesn't require marriage to make it either meaningful or enjoyable.

However, as long as we make children, some type of family is necessary. Marriage joins the work, and the joys, and the sadnesses of life for two partners. The family neither exists nor evolves in isolation: it has older family behind it, and a young family ahead. The family structure must allow for change, learning, and growth—or it dies.

At present, anxiety about marriage and family is almost universal. On every hand, one sees nervous concern over teenage marriage, infidelity, divorce, loosening sex standards, women's lib, momism, the decline of parental authority, the anarchy of youth, and so on. One senses deepening disillusion—even despair—surrounding the value of family life.

How could it be otherwise? The turbulence of contemporary society aggravates the built-in ambivalence of marriage. The quality of male-female partnership is tentative and transient. In a society stripped of tradition, wracked with conflict, and providing no accurate prediction of tomorrow, human relations at all levels are in a state of disequilibrium.

Three generations survey the record with dismay. The older folks look down on the younger with silent reproach. The younger marrieds look at themselves shocked and bewildered, wondering how they got this way. Children look at their parents, not with respect, but with disdain and bitter accusation. They seem to say: *"As partners in marriage and parenthood, your life is a lie. You betray yourselves; you betray us. Our family is turning into a tragic failure."*

I am a psychiatrist who has devoted a lifetime to studying emotional problems of family living. I have pioneered in the field of family therapy. From where I sit, the picture of marriage and family in present-day society is a gloomy one. Family life seems to be cracking at the seams, and an effective mortar is nowhere available.

The testimony of experts concerning change in the styles of marriage and family is admittedly paradoxical. It gravitates to two poles:

a) The family is changing but there is no need for alarm; it is merely retooling for the "new society."
   What new society? I ask.

b) The family is failing; it is no longer equipped to do its job for society. It

is virtually bankrupt. It is a defunct
social institution that has outlived its
usefulness.

At a recent symposium on "Man and Civilization:
The Family's Search for Survival," [1] there was a sharp
polarization of opinion. Some held that the family,
despite stress and strain, is thriving. Others asserted
that the family is showing signs of progressive dis-
organization and decay.

Parsons speaks of the "disintegration of transition."
Mead declares that the family flourishes as we change
from a "postconfigurational" family into a "preconfigur-
ational" one.

Burgess characterizes the changes as:

1) A downgrading of the authority of
   parents.

2) A trend toward equalitarianism in the
   relations between male and female,
   with a relative decrease in the authority of the male.

3) Parental uncertainty.

4) Decline in the importance of grand-
   parents.

5) The irresponsibility of children.

[1] Man and Civilization: The Family's Search for Survival - edited by
Seymour M. Farber, Piero Mustacchi, Roger H. L. Wilson -
McGraw Hill, 1965

Burgess interprets this transformation as a movement toward a companionship unit.

Merton asserts that "The alleged breakdown of family has been found to be specious rather than real." I cannot agree with this judgement.

The social scientist interprets family breakdown in one way; the psychiatrist, in another. The social scientist bases his studies on averages; the psychiatrist examines family breakdown in the context of individual case studies.

In some quarters, the psychiatrist is charged with "a need to see the whole community as a mental hospital." But, I ask, how many families do you know that you would call "normal and healthy"? How many marriages do you see that are happy and fulfilling?

Coffin[2] writes as follows:

It has become impossible for a lot of American families to live together. Some share the same roof, and nothing else. This disintegration of the home is a world-wide phenomenon, but the symptoms are most acute in our own materialist-militarist society.

Toffler[3] says:

Seventy years ago, when people got married to death do us part, that meant 30 years. Today, with the increased life span, it means 50 years, on the average. We are

2. 3 Look Magazine - January 26, 1971

> *clinging to traditional assumptions in the*
> *face of a fundamental change, and now*
> *expect people to make it together for two*
> *generations instead of one—a rather as-*
> *tonishing bit of optimism. We are moving*
> *toward a society based on temporary re-*
> *lationships rather than permanent.*

Thus, many social scientists concede that the family has lost its function as a unit of work, of protection, of education, of religious and recreational practices. Yet, they insist, that the family preserves its function as an affectional unit; that the family remains the psychic agency of society; that it socializes the child; that it stabilizes the adult; that it conserves our culture; and that it is the matrix for the development of personality. Certainly the family ought to be doing these things, but is it?

For example, the sociologist Otto Pollack believes that the family of the future may be the one force to save man from the increasing complexities of bureaucratic existence. Only the family will provide psychological relief as each person's life becomes more and more determined by impersonal forces.

Struggling with the dangers of the wider world, a person craves togetherness and turns back to his family for a sense of belonging and security.[4] Within the

---

[4] See: Ackerman, Nathan W. - The Psychodynamics of Family Life - Basic Books, 1958 Ackerman, Nathan W. - Treating the Troubled Family - Basic Books, 1966

family nest, each seeks to affirm a sense of personal dignity. But the present-day family is, in fact, poorly equipped to provide genuine belonging. In place of the real thing, one finds a trumped-up, artificial together-ness. Comes the family dinner at Christmas time, there is often a classic contagion of depression. And as the force of family tradition weakens, the influence of peer culture takes over. The aged are left isolated, as the youth destroy the unit.

Thus, the malady of the modern family shows in several ways:

1) A lack of consensus on values.

2) A pervasive sense of powerlessness.

3) Chronic immaturity with inability to assume effective responsibility.

4) Discontinuity and incongruity in the relations between family and society.

In the extreme, it appears as if each person goes his or her own way. The family of our day is a non-viable entity. As a form of organization, it is short-lived; it erases itself.[5] Any spontaneous healing is incomplete and twisted, lagging far behind the disintegrative forces. As the family struggles to adapt to a cataclys-mically changing society, a terrible toll is exacted in

[5] See: Birdwhistell, Raymond - The Idealized Model of the American Family, Social Casework, April 1970 - Vol. 51, No. 4

terms of damage to the social and emotional well-being of its members.

Common manifestations of marital disorder are:

1) Failure of reciprocal satisfaction.

2) Competitiveness.

3) Conflict and hostility.

4) Defective problem solving.

Husband and wife trap themselves in a vicious cycle of bickering and blaming. They lose the dignity of the passionate fight and the making-up kiss. In such a relationship, there is little joining of sex and affection. Too often, intercourse is cold, impersonal, frustrating; after the act, each partner feels even more alone than before.

The quality of competitiveness is demoralizing, each harboring an attitude of *What's in it for me?* The partnership is juggled as if the profit for one is the loss for the other. The nourishing spiritual side of companionship fades; in its place is a creeping loss of hope and trust. The couple can no longer feel together, talk together, play and work together. By degrees, mistrust, fear, and anger induce the conviction of aloneness. Marriage becomes disillusion, despair, and finally divorce.

It is currently fashionable to highlight "failures of communication." This puts the cart before the horse. Communication was invented to serve human beings, not the other way around. The real illness is not the inability to talk, but rather the progressive loss of kindness and empathy. If the partners could but feel, they would also talk.

A few clinical vignettes: Mr. and Mrs. X had been married one year. She wished for an exclusive commitment from her husband, but he insisted on the privilege of having affairs. For two or three weeks at a time they got along, but then they would quarrel explosively. The wife sought to impose feelings of loyalty. "Every time I see him, I want sex. I use him." When she applied pressure, however, she alienated him. For a time, he would baby her; but then he, too, would erupt with rage.

This couple knew one another for six years and broke up their courtship a number of times. During periods of separation, the wife slept with other men. She experienced orgasm only with her husband, but he remained hostile and alienated. This is an example of an immature, noncommitted marriage.

Another husband and wife were viewed publicly as an "ideal couple." They belonged to the local club, surrounded themselves with a network of friends. But, in fact, the relations of husband and wife were rotting. When interviewed, the husband was perplexed, frightened, but helpless to change the situation. The wife felt the marriage was a mistake. She did not love him, could not even feel him. Their life together was one long, boring routine. Their sexual life, too, lacked any closeness or affection. Fleeting affairs had only deepened the wife's sense of defeat. Despite all the motions of building home and family, these two people were completely out of touch. Four years later, they divorced. The wife returned to her own parents and gave the children to her husband. "I feel too immature and inadequate to care for them. I just don't feel the children."

In another "successful" family, the husband started out as a poor boy with an insatiable drive to succeed. He married a rich man's daughter and climbed the business ladder. He was a millionaire at 48; but privately, he was miserable. In business, he had a tiger by the tail, driven continuously to expand lest competitors plunge him to the bottom. At home, he was a shadow, forcing himself through the motions of family duties. It was a rich, comfortable but hollow way of life; a well-oiled routine, but without heart. He and his wife felt nothing for each other, yet acted as if they were close and loyal. They mutually denied the emptiness of their relationship, though rarely joining sexually. The void of feeling was too painful for them to face.

In this family, the children echoed the alienation of their parents. The eldest, a boy of 18, was a star athlete, driven in sports as his father was in business. But the boy, a school drop-out, could neither read nor spell. The younger children were extremely anxious, immature, and rivalrous, and had difficulty in making friends.

These examples point up the initial failure to marry

well, the defective capacity of the family members to heal conflict, and the contagion of warped values spreading to the children.

I have emphasized the most striking characteristic of marital failure as being progressive alienation of the partners. Alienation has two meanings. In one sense, the term refers to feelings of estrangement or detachment from self or from others; in another sense, alienation implies a trend toward depersonalization, toward a state of mind approaching insanity. This dual connotation has a special significance in marital relations: a loss of feeling for the partner is accompanied by a loss of feeling for the self. By stages, this moves towards feelings of emptiness, meaninglessness, loneliness, despair, deadness—ultimately, a loss of values and a loss of self. As the relationship is dehumanized, one or both partners may suffer a breakdown. The incidence of mental illness, delinquency, and addiction in alienated persons is conspicuously higher than in a stable family; the rate of suicide is three times as high.

For every couple that enters the divorce courts, there are uncounted numbers that remain under one roof and continue in the chronic agony of emotional divorce. In a mood of quiet desperation, the partners hang together rather than hang separately, while continuously sharing the contagion of pain, humiliation, and isolation. In the study and treatment of emotionally disabled families, one observes that alienation and emotional disturbance in one member of the marital pair predictably lead to similar trends in the other. It is not only that "the sick marry the sick"; it is also true that the sick make each other sicker.

Today, there is one divorce for every three marriages. In 70 years, the rate has risen 450%. Legal divorce, however, is the end result; emotional divorce is the primary condition. Let us not forget Schopenhauer's parable.

There is a streak of divorce in every family. Alienation of husband and wife breeds alienation of parent and grandparent, parent and child, also alienation of the family from the surrounding community. Divorce negates marriage; but alienation and atomization of family relationships negate life itself.

I have emphasized and illustrated three core processes:

1) Alienation of the lone individual and the lone family.

2) Contagion of anxiety rendering family members susceptible to breakdown.

3) Social and emotional disturbances in the family unit emerging in identifiable clusters.

In a time of revolution, how is the family affected by the crumbling of old cultural forms and the emergence of new standards? How shall we interpret the changed and changing relations of male and female? One cannot fail to be impressed by the acceleration of all stages of male-female interaction: boy-girl parties, dancing, dating, "going steady," and sexual experimentation. Children seem to be catapulted into a premature maturity." [6]

Along the path of loosening sex standards, we come to "shacking up," the living together of unwed couples, unmarried motherhood, the matriarchal type family, group sex, group marriages, the commune. I have previously indicated a clinical example of immature marriage. Premature parenthood is its inevitable complication. As a possible antidote, Margaret Mead had suggested "marriage in two steps"—individual and parental. The former entails a minimum of mutual responsibility; it is easily dissolved. Lasting commitment is reserved for a later parental marriage.

At first glance, separation of the sexual contract from the parental contract is attractive. It seems to satisfy the radicalism of free sexual choice for young couples and the conservative needs of parenthood. Ostensibly, it would support the virtues of freedom, flexibility, and adventure in the lives of young people, while safeguarding the continuity of family across the generations. To the young, it offers a reassuring balm against the fright of marriage as a trap.

But is it natural to divorce sexual union from parenthood? In my opinion, this is an error. There is an appropriate level of responsibility in sexual union, how-

[6] Thomas, Rachelle: "Is Sex Morality Out of Date," Child & Family, Vol. 5, No. 2, 1966

ever different it might be from that of parental union.

Mead's proposal offers the lure of having one's cake and eating it, too. Instead of enhancing the intimacy and commitment of male and female, her scheme may paradoxically aggravate the trend toward transient, superficial relationships. Marriage and family are grown-up business, not kid stuff.

It is easy to understand the frantic sex-seeking of lonely young people as a protest against alienation, anxiety, and spiritual bankruptcy in adult relationships; but this sex-seeking should not be transformed into a social program. "Marriage in two steps"—rather than tackling underlying causes—seems to yield to the turbulence and immaturity of youth.

With respect to changing sex practices, we note an additional paradox: less social constraint on the one hand, but reinforced inner constraint on the other. The youth talk a good line, but do not feel as sexually released as they would like to believe. After each roll in the hay, an agonizing loneliness may overtake the participants. Emotional intimacy did not arrive with orgasm. Again and again, one hears from young people that sexual adventure is an empty thing, far inferior to a heart-warming rap session. They are learning that there cannot be sexual freedom without genuine closeness, and a responsible caring for the partner.

In the counter culture of youth, there are the seeds of a new morality; a joining of love and sex; a striving for intimacy, sharing, loyalty and cooperation; a quest for honesty, dignity, and spiritual integrity in human relations; a yearning for freedom coupled with the assumption of interpersonal responsibility; a commitment to non-violence. The values and strivings of youth are being progressively politicized; but youth is youth—naive, impulsive, and lacking in a seasoned wisdom in the ways of man. Youth cannot make it alone. There must be a new joining of father and son, of mother and daughter, and of husband and wife.

The changes in the style of relations of male and female are part of the zeitgeist. The emancipation of women could be a great humanizing force in our society. Yet, says Van Horne,[7] "This seems born, not of a wish to liberate women from drudgery and second class citizenship, but rather to even old scores with the male sex." The altered relations of male and female are locked to related social phenomena: the generation gap, the role of youth in the changing society, the disillusionment with the revolt against the Establishment. Clearly, the sexual revolution is inextricably intertwined with other expressions of dissent, such as dissent against war and against the materialistic, manipulative, hypocritical orientation of the older generation.

The widespread disorders of marriage and family are the expression of a clash between the goals and values of society and the goals and values of family living. Stripped of the needed societal protection, the integrity and continuity of family life are doubtful. Yet I fear that the death of the family would be the death

[7] Van Horne, Harriette: - N. Y. Post, April 1971

of our kind of civilization.

Beneath the turmoil, one senses potentials for healing: group action for social reform, the striving to build a better community, the involvement of youth in social change, a new kind of joining of whole families in the struggle with social disorders.

Despite my gloomy estimate of how most families function today, I must concede that it appears as if the family is here to stay. But to be a viable social unit, the family must find a creative rebirth. This can only happen within a larger change: a creative rebirth of the entire social community. We must bend our efforts to evolve within our universe human cells, teams, neighborhood groups which join people through common goals and activities. Within such groups, we must nurse and evolve a new kind of connectedness and human caring.

The family is experimenting with new forms. Up to this moment, the new designs for family living do not provide a viable alternative. But barring the holocaust of total war, one may yet hope for a renascence.

Born, educated, and still residing in New York City, Marya Mannes is best known as an author, a critic, and a free-lance magazine writer. She has also written satirical light verse, and appears frequently as a TV commentator.

From 1952 until the fall of 1963, she was on the staff of THE REPORTER, *writing television and theatre criticism, social comment, and special features.*

Miss Mannes' published works include the novels MESSAGE FROM A STRANGER, *and* THEY. *Her collections of essays are* MORE IN ANGER, BUT WILL IT SELL? *and* THE NEW YORK I KNOW. *National Educational Television produced her script of* THEY *in April, 1970.*

Articles by Miss Mannes have appeared in THE NEW YORK TIMES, MCCALL'S, TV GUIDE, *as well as in other national publications.*

Marya Mannes

CONFRONTED WITH CONTRARY EVIDENCE, the adversary position against marriage is hard to maintain. The sight of a man's and a woman's relishing their thirtieth anniversary in the company of those they love; the way two beautiful young people look at each other when they say "I do!"; the touch of a husband's hand on his wife's shoulder. . . To maintain—in the face of these and many other instances of the special tenderness of married companionship and continuity—that the institution of marriage has reached the end of its human usefulness is both difficult and contradictory.

Yet prolonged observation, personal experience, and accumulated thought has brought some of us to believe that marriage now is only for the very rare or the very ordinary. The rare are those men and women who find in each other their complete emotional, intellectual, and spiritual complements and who were lucky enough to meet in the first place.

The ordinary are those of small aspirations, imagination, or curiosity: the passive who find contentment within the frame of habit and tradition.

For the majority who are neither rare nor ordinary, marriage may no longer be the answer, even though this arrangement between man, woman, and family has worked for so many centuries as a practical, productive, and often happy equation.

Yet more and more people now seriously question its validity. Why? Because one out of every three marriages dissolves in divorce? Because the infidelities of husband or wife are increasingly common? Because so many of the young are finding other ways to live together and love one another without sanction of church or state?

All these.

Good marriages, long marriages still exist, through a combination of consistent mutual need, compatibility, and love. They can exist until death even through need alone: the accretion of habits without which both mates are lost. Bad marriages can last through guilt alone.

But marriage itself is, I believe, a casualty of time: not only because of its own span between man and woman, but because of the point in time now reached in history.

For centuries, marriage has rested and survived on a common basis of assumptions as well as needs. That the needs no longer match the assumptions seems clear to those whose own marriages have not only failed but who see around them the wreckages of other marriages which appeared "ideal." The shock of discovering that A and B—"the perfect couple"—have parted is now a social cliché.

We have grown to accept the fact, reluctantly, that very little is as it seems; and that there may indeed be a basic and serious flaw in the concept that a man and a woman should be expected to love or honor each other, let alone live with each other, for forty or more years.

That so many have done so, even without love or respect or desire, until death—long after their children were raised, long after real communication ceased— was due partly to religious precept and social acceptance but mainly to lack of alternatives.

Wherever in this world certain factors still exist, there is still no choice. Isolation, poverty, ignorance, lack of outside communications, and, above all, laws made by men and upheld by men, in the name of the State or in the name of God, still determine the inexorable yoke: marriage for life in the eyes of God, for the service of the State, for the protection of woman, for the convenience of man, for the breeding of children. These are the societies which are still light-years away from the huge urban centers and technologized nations of the new world we inhabit.

Yet even we—so-called civilized, so-called developed—are only just beginning to question, in the name of our constitutional rights, how seriously these laws of men and priests have infringed on and limited the individual rights of men and women. We are only just beginning to suggest that they have no business at all in our private relationships.

Whatever its trivial and loveless aspects may be, the sexual revolution has clearly established the inherent right of man and woman over the disposition of their own bodies and the fulfillment of their own desires, so long as these desires do not violate the rights of others. How heterosexuals or homosexuals choose to love one another or live with each other is their determination alone. Whether a woman chooses to bear or not to bear a child is her decision alone. Neither state nor church has any rights in this choice. Whether a man and a woman choose to marry or not to marry depends on their mutual desire. The length of their union may be determined not only by the duration of their love but on the nurturing of such children as they have chosen to bear. Here, and only here, it would seem that some contractual form could be introduced to assure the equal responsibility of both parents in the care and instruction of their children until they reached maturity. Since maturity is now attained at an earlier age than ever before, a couple marrying in their twenties would presumably have discharged this obligation (or more likely, have been discharged from it!) by their late thirties or early forties, leaving them twenty years in which to exercise alternative choices: to continue together, or to choose other partners, or to lead single lives.

Ironically, the ties of traditional marriage now break much sooner, leaving children split between parents, and parents split by the ignominies and ugliness of divorce. There is no more assurance in marriage now for family continuity than there would be on a contractual "partnership" basis; and probably less. There might, indeed, be more if a communal pattern could be established in which—as in the Israeli kibbutz —parents and children remain a family unit within a broader framework: where both adults and children share common tasks, pleasures, and responsibilities.

I have come to believe that the small, single-family unit—whether urban or suburban—contributes most to the death of marriage as we have known it and literally "locks in" not only man and wife, but also child and parent, allowing neither to develop freely and fully as individuals.

The almost universal pattern of absent husband and home-bound wife for nine or ten hours of every week-day can often, I suspect, be disastrous for both. It is based, of course, on the classic premise that it is the man's role to go out and earn the support of his family, while it is the woman's role to clean the house, feed the family, and raise their children. His job may be a meaningless and draining grind; his daily commuting, a double torture; and her total absorption in child-care or housekeeping and the company of other women, a wasting confinement. With luck and during a limited span of desire, however, they might consider themselves happily married. Millions probably still do.

But when the distraction of children ends and husband and wife are left alone together with ebbing desire and few mutual interests, what happens then? What point has their union if he still works all day (meeting new people, at least, facing new challenges) and she is bereft of function or resources? Do bridge and community activities and occasional hobbies really fill the gap? Does companionship limited to a few evening hours and weekends, does habit itself, really constitute a full life for a human being with the capacity for wider options?

Apparently, they still do for those men—and especially for those women—who find security and safety within the limitations of long familiarity. Options can be frightening to the naturally dependent and to the unimaginative. And millions of women, who would deny that they are either, still claim that they find total fulfillment as home-makers, wives, and mothers. More power to them if they do, even if the price of their fulfillment is the death by continuous strain of the men who provided it; even if the price be their own long widowhood.

The total support of wives and families, moreover, is as much a deterrent to men's liberation as human beings as the total dependence of women impedes their own. The trap of office can be as confining as the trap of home; and both contribute to a sterility of atmosphere which has unquestionably been a root-cause for the flight of the young from the patterns that created those traps.

For too many years the term "dominating" has been confined to the independent woman with a life and goals of her own. It could far more accurately describe the full-time housewife whose dominant presence in the home as the controlling parent can cause— and often does cause—long-term harm to her young.

A father, usually drained in the evenings, a father, usually needing his weekend leisure to find physical relief in pursuits of his own, is not father enough to redress the vital parental balance. And it is no wonder that the products of this imbalance are seeking another way out. Not only in drugs—which are no answer except negation—but in the free coming-together of man and woman as sharing mates: sharing tasks, sharing earnings, sharing, equally, the nurture of their young. In the breaking down of their parents' patterns, these young people may find that the concept of marriage itself is meaningless.

If there is a real commitment to one another in the fullest sense, no authority is needed to license it or validate it. If the commitment ends by mutual consent or by single desire, no license can renew it. A marriage contract, then, becomes the social shield of two unhappy people, or is replaced by the tortuous legalities of divorce.

Present divorce laws, moreover, are flagrantly anti-male in the matter of alimony. The support of dependent children is one thing. The support of a woman physically and mentally able to work, after the time needed for her to find other means of support, is not only an unfair burden on the man but an added spur to female indolence and dependence.

Alimony for some women may be sheer necessity: the result of long dependence in which no individual skills or talents have been developed for use in the world outside. But alimony for many women is often a form of revenge, a sheer rapacity: a rather unattractive emotion. This is the expected product of the marriage-divorce pattern which fosters a bitterness out of proportion to the human failings which have pulled apart two people who once were together.

Now, after the convulsions of the last ten years, the pattern seems as archaic as the whale-bone corset, as meaningless as the term *premarital sex*, as anachronistic as the marriage announcements in the daily papers: the smiling young brides-to-be, the pedigreed grooms, the hint of finality and bliss. Weddings in churches, weddings under tents, weddings in homes and gardens. Visions of little houses and little children. Tears at the ceremony. A lovely ritual, replaced three or four or five years later, likely enough, by unritual tears or recriminations in a lawyer's office.

If this seems cynical, the cynicism is directed not at the joining in life of two people, young or older, who believe they have found unity in each other. It is directed against the official, social, and public sanction of a private deed, a private commitment.

It is also an extenuation of an ancient and, in my opinion, humiliating deed of ownership. In return for the love, protection, and support from a man, a woman surrenders her name and her identity to her husband —taking his. The day before, she is a human being called Mary Smith: an individual. The day after, she is Mrs. William Jones: a wife. But Bill Jones, whether he wears a ring or not, remains Bill Jones forever: Mr. Jones, as before. Without a ring, he bears no label of contract. But Mrs. Jones, wherever she goes, does. The world is told she belongs to him.

And whether she knows it or not, it is the first step

of an inner as well as outer dependence in which she comes to live not only *on* him, but *through* him.

In surrendering her public identity, she can come to forfeit her private self. Living on his money, rising and falling with his successes or failures, she is, as wife, accessory to his fact.

What man would tolerate a contract by which he were to cede his name and identity to the woman he marries, adopting hers? It would seem to me not only a prime psychological but legal goal of women's liberation to give this ancient seal of male ownership and female surrender a decent burial at long last. And even if the public form of marriage still persists, to assure that not one but both partners alike retain their names, as human beings do in any other contract or commitment joining two individuals into one entity.

The obvious question immediately arises: what of the children? Whose name, what name, shall they bear?

Does it matter? Can they not choose their surnames as they now choose everything else in their lives? And if some of them should still value some kind of continuity, some tangible inheritance of family identity, why not the mother's instead of the father's, as his or her option? Why should only Queens be allowed to preserve their blood-lines as well as Kings?

Besides which, this is now a world of Tim and Joan and Mark and Lynn. The Mr. and Mrs. parade is on its way out except in older circles where the stultifying arrangement of married couples is supposed to constitute a party. Parties are celebrations of individuals coming together and meeting each other, and the matter of who "belongs" to whom can be sorted out by those who care more about forms than substance.

We have been, for that matter, perhaps the most over-domesticated society in the world in this matter of coupling. The single woman over twenty-five is suspect; the unmarried woman over forty, pitied. A man not married at thirty is thought to be either homosexual or at least "peculiar," although the social value of the bachelor (*any* single male of *any* age) is infinitely higher than that of any single woman, however attractive. The rigidity of this pattern in conventional circles is only too well known by the mateless woman: one more proof that her social value is determined not by her qualities or contributions as a human being but by the husband she provides for table seating.

This couple-obsession has never existed among creative people simply because they live intensely individual lives as men and women, married or not. Their gatherings are heterogeneous in the matter of sex and age and talents, as well as in life patterns. Their natures abhor the vacuum of convention, even though they observe the manners of hospitality. And even while, as in every human group, there is the familiarity of old ties and friendships, the mixture is leavened by single men and women: new explorations, new combinations, new discoveries.

This is an international society, immediately recognized in every country's creative or cultural core, whether of art or science. It is the kind of free society the young think they have discovered, but have actually only enlarged in the sense of numbers; and in so doing, possibly diminished. Their obsessive need for crowd-movement constitutes a conformity in clear opposition to the individuality of the creative few.

But at least they have broken down the stifling patterns of conventional pairing in their recognition of love as infinitely variable: love as a freeing as well as a binding agent, love incompatible with the concept of possession.

Many of the young are marrying, will marry. Many still cannot shake off their early maternal conditioning as easily as they think. Girls groomed to be brides from the age of eight onwards, boys conditioned to take care of them or make use of them. Both envisioning marriage as the dispeller of loneliness and alienation.

Nor can they shake off years of another conditioning: the television images which they may consciously scorn and reject, but which have drummed into their ears and eyes for two decades the mythology of sex-love-marriage as the indivisible trinity: solving all problems, promising fulfillment.

Since then, of course, the counter-culture of film and theatre and rock has demolished these myths, substituting new myths in which drugs, and sex, and sound, and movement are the magic agents of communion through common sensation.

And even that most potent mirror of middle-class

attitudes—commercial TV—has brought to millions of people all over the world the constant availability of other options. Middle-aged husbands in small mid-Western towns, in New Hampshire villages, in Southern hamlets can see the swinging young beauties that freer men enjoy; and their wives, looking at the lean sexuality of their young male counterparts, wonder what all the wedlocked years have robbed them of.

In the bigger towns and cities, the pornie houses and even the major cinemas show every form of sexual coupling and group erotica. And although off-screen husbands and wives, who now feel free to enjoy these new experiences with other couples, claim that the variety enhances rather than hurts their own marriages, the final returns may sharply question the claim.

For the essence, reason, and force of marriage rests on monogamy, or at least on the belief in monogamy. The contract is one of mutual trust and honor, or it is invalid. If love is constant, the occasional brief lapse in trust can be forgiven, if not forgotten. A good marriage may sustain small deceptions, but the fabric is steadily weakened by continuing ones. Whether the bond is strong enough for a husband and wife who find more pleasure in the bodies of others, openly as well as secretly, is, I think, very doubtful. Then the private intimacies and delights that forged the marriage ties no longer exist.

The appetite for sexual variety has always been acknowledged as a deep male drive, indulged in most societies as a matter of course—in marriage or out, openly or in secret.

Now it has at last become abundantly clear—and acknowledged—that the female appetite is equally powerful. Neither may surface in the early years of a marriage which satisfies both. But there seems little question that long familiarity is both counter-erotic and counter-productive. This may not matter deeply in men and women closely bound by other ties of mind and spirit, of respect and affection. But it matters deeply to the sexually vigorous, who might formerly have reined themselves in and born their frustrations either as a marital duty or as the common condition. How many millions of house-bound women have not suffered it through how many thousands of years? Men too, of course. But there were whores and "loose" girls, even in villages, for the men. And for women? Resignation, housework, farmwork, children.

Children. Why left to the last? Haven't children always been the reason, the purpose, the bond of marriage?

Up till now, indeed. But now, with the press of overpopulation as the major root of our major global ills, the family—for sheer human survival—must grow smaller and smaller. The consensus of those who study the ruinous abuse of this planet and the equally ruinous urban environments is two children at most, or zero population growth.

Two children, wanted, nurtured, freed when their wings are strong. But not the brood which used to make the family a self-contained community, which of necessity included mother and father as joint foundation and pediment.

But now, not even three or four or more children can hold together husband and wife. In fact, there are as many divorces between the parents of children as there are between childless couples.

This is not as strange as it might seem since a man and woman who have only each other often learn to know each other and need each other more intensely without the ever-conflicting loyalties and responsibilities toward the young. Instead, they develop themselves to their utmost capacities as human beings, free to engage in joint ventures of work or exploration, free to enlarge their horizons by travel and change of environments.

Among the happiest married couples I have known are professional men and women—scientists, doctors, lawyers, artists, teachers, musicians—who bring to their joint or different disciplines a constant interaction and stimulation. Whether their lack of children was the result of incapacity or deliberation is questioned only in traditional societies which brand them as "selfish."

At this stage of human evolution, on the contrary, they may be less selfish than the men and women who bear children for their own delight and as a perpetuation of their own lives. Now, at least and at last, the bearing of children is no longer the duty of women, for church, or for state. She is free to bear a child when she wants, and soon—if the Supreme Court of the United States decides to support the Constitution—free not to bear an unwanted child. The Court has repeatedly acknowledged "a 'right of privacy' or 'liberty' in matters related to marriage, family, and sex." This should inevitably include a woman's right to abortion.

Children, then, can no longer be regarded as the major argument for the present form of marriage as an institution required by the state and the church. That they must be included as the prime responsibility of their parents in any substitute agreement or contract between a man and a woman is self-evident.

But when children are grown and gone, the institution of marriage, as it now exists, can and does increasingly constrict the lives of a man and a woman who might each feel the need to lead a fuller or more vital existence without each other, and—more importantly— without the pain and destructiveness of divorce proceedings.

It is no crime to cease loving. It is more a crime to continue a marriage without love, without purpose, without communication. How many couples, still strong and active in middle years, are sitting in restaurants opposite each other, having nothing to say to each other? How many couples sit in cramped rooms looking at television, or on the porch looking at nothing? How many marriages are envelopes of hate, or boredom, or futility, or simply social convenience?

One might argue that these men and women might be no better off if they were not married. Perhaps. Perhaps they are "the ordinary," who really have no visions or desires.

But perhaps, too, they once had higher aspirations, but, unfortunately, watched them wither and die over the years before they ever had chance to take root and flower.

Perhaps the patterns of convenience are still worth this intangible loss. After all, the man has a free housekeeper, cook, and nurse. And the woman has a free roof over her head. But to many, the price of this "freedom" in the name of marriage is too high a price to pay.

Perhaps best known as a film and drama critic, Judith Crist calls the shots exactly as she sees them, immune to pressures from any source.

Since 1963, she has been a film and drama commentator of the NBC-TV Today Show, and is also currently active as film critic for TV GUIDE *and* NEW YORK *Magazine.*

She has received a spate of awards. In 1970, she was chosen as one of twelve alumnae to receive the Hunter College President's Medal for Distinguished Service—the highest award the college may bestow on its alumni.

A poll conducted by Louis Harris Associates found her to be the most influential film critic in the United States.

Her book, THE PRIVATE EYE, THE COWBOY AND THE VERY NAKED GIRL: MOVIES FROM CLEO TO CLYDE, *has been widely acclaimed.*

Judith Crist

THERE'S NOTHING WRONG with the asylum; it's the inmates who are going to pieces.

An unfortunate metaphor for marriage? It stems, I suspect, from the first "adult" joke (i.e. one that had to be explained) I remember, delivered by a baggy-pants comedian at a vaudeville in my childhood, that grand chestnut, "Marriage is a great institution—but who wants to live in an institution?"

Well, about 90 percent of the over-twenty population opts for marriage annually, as their ancestors have through the ages. And they always will, in that human continuum that insists on crying "Doom! Doom!" as surface life-styles *appear* to change every couple of decades. The world moves in circles and social habits with it; only the custom—or the label attached thereto—changes and the more it changes, as the French naturally would note, the more it's the same.

And certainly, "institution" or not, marriage is the most enduring of man's habits, creations, rituals, instincts, mythologies, indulgences, perversions, refuges —you name it. Civilizations have come and gone; from recorded history on, marriage survives. Debating its durability along with its pros and cons, therefore, may well seem on a par with rehashing the lurid to determine whether justice triumphed or manufacturing a topical "How I Found God while Spying for the FBI

with a Dog that had Peculiar Sex Habits," and offering
it, of course, to the READER'S DIGEST. (Who is without
sin? Freely I confess the most remunerative magazine
article I wrote in my nonspecialized youth was a survey
of early post-World War II G.I. marriages, entitled
"Why They Marry Foreign Women"—an article that was,
c.f. supra, very shrewdly retitled, when it was bought by
the READER'S DIGEST for republication in about 18 different languages, "Do Foreign Women Make Better
Wives?") But debate it we do—and, undoubtedly, will.

The stimulus to the debate for about the past
twenty or thirty years, it seems to me, has been that
hoary statistic that one (or more, depending on the
offerant's viewpoint) out of every four marriages ends
in divorce. Does this mean that every fourth marriage
is doomed or does it mean that for every four marriages performed one divorce decree is granted? After
all, consider how a *New York Times* reporter pepped
up the topic by discovering, back in 1966, that in
Los Angeles County there were four divorces *or annul-
ments* (italics mine) recorded to every five marriage
licenses issued. Is marriage going to hell? Or could it
possibly be that divorce is getting to be a hell of a
lot easier?

There are, as we were overly fond of noting archly
during the interscholastic debates of our youth, lies—
damned lies—and statistics. And we shall eschew them.
After all, Vance Packard—and I choose him as a quintes-
sential example of the popular sex-marriage researcher
—devoted four years to international investigation,

consulted with more than 300 sociologists, psychologists, educators, clergymen, doctors, and other "experts," and in 1968 came up with THE SEXUAL WILDERNESS, a 553-page concensus replete with some 400 reference notes, lush appendices, and a fat index—and very little that anyone with common sense doesn't know. And his conclusion, after all the hashing and rehashing of statistical studies, was that marriage, "a process of fulfilling, unifying and recreating," remains for the majority, throughout the ages, "still the ultimate of attainment."

Common sense would indicate, from those divorce statistics, that there's nothing wrong with marriage. The problem lies with the people who get married. And certainly, for whatever involved sociological and psychological reasons that hold true in the past and the present and assuredly the future, people get married for all the wrong reasons, indicating that they have no clear idea of what marriage is all about.

Shall we belatedly define terms? Are we talking of the conjunction of true minds? In those terms, several homosexual couples I know are the best and most happily married among us. Are we talking about a legalism, a formal contract? Let's settle somewhere in between, facing the fact that individually we are bound by our upbringing, our traditions, our conditioning, our social environment, our psyche. Ideally, we should be talking of that marriage of true minds, of two people who decide to join together because their individual lives are bettered and their joint life a satisfying one.

And because our society requires a formal contract for certain benefits (ranging from joint tax returns to social acceptance within some communities to simply making it easier for your friends to address Christmas cards to you) the true minds usually have the common sense to go through the legal ritual, just as they don't drive around without a driver's license or, on certain social levels, with their two front teeth missing. Should those true minds mature together—there seems to me a natural growth, from lovers to spouses, to progenitors, to parents, as enrichment of the individual life through the joint one—and have children, the legalism is again an asset, making life for the child easier, again within the strictures of the society we choose to function in.

That, essentially, is what marriage is all about—although certainly you'd never guess it from the images provided generation after generation. In our male-dominated civilization—and let me emphasize that chauvinist pigs of both sexes have kept civilization that way—marriage was, and continues to be, a purely economic-survival refuge for women. And the American woman has loved it this way, despite the rantings of the feminine mystiquers who are a passing fad of the radical chic of our days. The woman who has wanted to be liberated has had the door open since the turn of the century, even longer.

We're a couple of centuries away from the time when the only alternatives to marriage were the convent or the whorehouse. Certainly during the 20th century, the American woman has learned to become the parasite supreme, offering ungenerous helpings of sexuality and fertility in exchange for not merely survival, but more often—and obviously I am speaking of the middle-class woman—luxury in a gadget-ridden "prison" that has left her free to sit on her backside and bemoan her lot. And how nice of all those Women's Lib free spirits to give her the further consolation of thinking how she could be a doctor, a lawyer, or an Indian chief if only it weren't for this white male tyrant who's been feeding, housing and supporting her and flatteringly regarding her as a sex object, no less!

This "sex object" shtick is just another inexplicable bit of the jargon that goes on to attack marriage as a call for role-playing or for the sacrifice of one's "identity." You are what you are—and not what you eat or what you sleep with. Who can keep a straight face watching all these radical chicks—so devotedly doing their own thing that they all manage to look alike, as all their male counterparts seem to do, too—objecting to construction workers' whistles (why shouldn't the great unwashed do their thing, if it's only to say, in effective whistle inarticulation, "Me Tarzan, you Jane, and it's nice we're both alive at the same time"?) or blaming their own failure to raise themselves above "object" status on the state of our society. Face it: object is as object does.

At any rate, our society, while establishing marriage as a money deal for women, has insisted on romanticizing it—much in the same way women insist on romanticizing their sexuality in their self-conviction that lust must be called "love." In effect, we have been told that if we stick to the legal rules, we will be rewarded; if we don't play the legal game—pow! The message, carried loud and clear via the mass media, has been with us for the past forty years, first from Hollywood and then, when it plunged into its era of plastic smut to outrace the competition, from television.

Marriage, and marriage alone, provided all the SEX—OOPS—LOVE you wanted; extramarital, let alone premarital, sex—oops—love led to nothing but frustration and misery at best, more often to sudden death or slow dying. All the fun and games came beforehand, of course: boy got girl only at fadeout time in the comedies.

Up to the mid-60's, the message about the rewards was subtle, sex-wise; we were left to imagine what spouses did as, fully-nightclothed and tucked into their twin beds, they clasped hands across the night table while hubby, with lecherous grin, turned out the light. And even those who felt we came from un-chic or impoverished homes because the parental bed was double rather than twinned were overcome by the romanticism of it all. Of course, in the smut era that was the media's interpretation of an "honest" or "open" approach to sex, marriage was reduced to a naked wallow on a mattress, shoulder to heaving shoulder, with orgasmic gasps on the soundtrack.

But the ultimate message was that in exchange for her virginity a woman would, by contract, get the material things of life and, if she bitched enough, she'd get better and better ones as time went by. And who but the women of America to whom the movies are primarily addressed and who are the backbone of television's situation-drama-comedy corps, have heartily endorsed this myth? It wasn't the men who worshipped Doris Day right down to her last evasion on the sofa in her career-girl films or her diaphanous-nightied romp in that exquisite all-electric mile-wide ranch house that marriage provided as a matter of course.

What you see is what you get—and that's the purchase American men and women have been agreeing on, little realizing that what they see is not what they'll be getting in five, ten or twenty years. What they see is usually a sex object—male as well as female—and, because of that puritanical and hypocritical heritage that dominates too many lives, lust is quickly put into romantic terms, and the contract undertaken. Those who marry for sexual satisfactions are in the same time-capsule as those who've made the money deal; inevitably a time comes when the deal isn't what it used to be. At that point, of course, we enter into other Marriage-Manual-Type Problems, wherefor the "experts" discuss games, whether man (why not woman?) is polygamous, whether double standards are the going thing. Nonsense. Marriages founded on rotten reasons—money and sex—are bound to founder.

That all-American hunger for money, for an economic and social security that marriage can bring, has, I suspect, been outclassed in recent years by the all-American orgasm hang-up as the prime reason for marital rot. All the pop lit emphasis on sexual performance and sexual satisfaction has led to the concept of marriage as a sexual olympiad, a competitive arena where no activity counts off the mattress, and no emotional response exists above the groin.

And these have led to "role playing," to a fakery and a substitution of all sorts of false values in what was intended simply as a human relationship, a compact between two individuals who have found that being together, as Pishna said, is almost as good as being alone and, in some respects, even better. Basically, the only reason to enter into such a partnership is that without it an individual's life is less, its fulfilment impossible, its dreams unattainable. And that takes a long-term view.

But we are in an age of conspicuous consumption, where there is a built-in obsolescence in most things, a planned obsolescence for others. And marriage has been fitted into the pattern. Just as divorce laws began to be humanized to correct the mistakes of marriages undertaken for the wrong reasons, so further wrong reasoning entered into marriage. Better wed than— well, not dead, but virginal; better a divorcee than an old maid, since statistics showed . . . . and, above all, if at first you don't succeed. . . .

This attitude seemed to me most prevalent among the newly married of the 50's, when the so-called silent generation found self-expression in early marriage, in early parenthood and in divorce. (Ours was the so-called deprived generation that married in the 40's, when Depression childhoods had made the girls career-conscious and World War II combined with that experience to make the boys security-conscious, and when planned parenthood was the order of the intellectual's day.) But it is prevalent today, at least among that segment of the young not left totally cynical by the marital rot around them. But the cynicism is an indication of the utter romanticism of their concept of marriage. After all, only those with illusions can have them shattered; only those with inflated ideals can have them deflated.

So let's take the illusions and the pink clouds away from our concept of what marriage is really about. It's not a lifetime love affair; it's not a business arrangement; it's not a foster-parent plan. It is only a matter of two individuals leading their own and their mutual lives with a full realization that they both will change with time and experience and that they will have to accept and to agree to these changes. That takes a lot of thought and anticipation, but these are the prerequisites for a lasting marriage.

It takes a thorough knowledge of every possible aspect of the partner—and the partnership. With these, how can a woman feel that a "role" has been foisted upon her? Didn't she agree to take a part in the play—and wasn't the part discussed or considered before the contract was signed? How can there be the surprise of infidelity—if the question of fidelity were put into an agreed-upon context? How can there be a question of parental responsibilities, if parenthood has been considered as part of the deal?

How inarticulate this age of "utter frankness" is!

With all the touching and the feeling and the en-
countering that goes on, with all the blather about a
sexual revolution, we're really in the same cycle of thirty
and forty years ago. The only difference is that nowadays we pretend that we are "utterly frank," that we've
discovered a new and better "life style." Ah yes, today's
liberated lady insists she'll bring up her son without
benefit of wedlock or a paternal presence; wait until
she faces the small problem of getting him off the potty
and teaching him to urinate standing up! Or am I
dated and is unisex supposed to do away with that
difference? I cite this homely but rather typical facet
of life-without-father only because our relatively late-
in-life child was in nursery school with a whole crop
of mid-50's kiddies whose parents divorced right after
their birth, and my husband was called upon by a
number of the ungay divorcées to help out with the
problem.

Marriage, in the full partnership sense, does have
its uses, even beyond the joint raising of children who
need the masculine and feminine affections and guid-
ance that the professionals—nursemaids, teachers, whatever—cannot give them. Marriage remains the stronghold
of individualism, of individuals joined. And, above all,
marriage is for grown-ups.

When you grow up, you discover that there are
people you like and people you love and people you
enjoy being with because they enhance your pleasure
and enrich your experience in a mutual activity—
whether it's movie-going, or skiing, or sex, or hiking, or

political activism, or whatever your interests include. (Nothing Freudian, my dear—I simply put sex in its proper perspective; some people see two or three movies a day; some see two or three a year.) And the lucky ones among us find someone we not only love but whom we also like, someone who enhances our life and shares our experiences and ambitions, who sympathizes and empathizes, and who has almost as many vices, vulnerabilities and vanities as we. And this is the adult mating game.

Its chances of success are improving steadily, for those of us who reinforce our luck with common sense. The bars are almost down on premarital sex—and chances are this will at least lower the percentage of boobies who think they have to tie themselves into marital knots for a tumble in the hay. Women's Lib is hopefully going to embarrass an increasing number of women into doing something with whatever talents they have for contributing to the world's work—and chances are this will decrease the number of women who attempt to turn marriage into a free lunch counter. And despite the pother in addressing envelopes or the doubtful looks from neanderthal neighbors, increasing numbers of young people are living together without benefit of clergy or label (and wouldn't they be irritated to be told how long ago the idea of "trial marriage" caused its public stir!), with the possibility somewhere on the horizon of legalizing their relationship. If they do, fine. If not, that's one divorce the fewer, a loss only to the doomsday statisticians.

Of course marriage, theoretically, can have small appeal for that generation of flower children dedicated to loving the whole world and too childish or too selfish to undertake the difficult task of loving one person. Just as well. As noted, marriage is for adults who not only will take a change for the worse but also can anticipate it, or at least its possibilities. Of course, familiarity over the years can breed contempt—but it can also breed an interdependence and an understanding. Who among us does not need the security of having someone before whom you can stand naked and unashamed? And I mean deep-down naked, even with all your clothes on. Marriage, in fact, is the last refuge of privacy in our drearily public society.

And hopefully, in our maturity, we can get away from the Maggie & Jiggs approach to marriage, let alone the mass media stereotypes. Again—and I suppose it takes a woman to be an anti-feminist—women have proved to be their own worst enemies, supporting by their purchases the products that choose to depict them as household slaves getting their ecstacies out of a highly polished floor and their orgasms from a foamy shampoo; seeing their males, whether spouse or child, as simple-minded slobs who contribute only dirty laundry to the home; regarding their daughters as stupids who must be taught not to sweat and which soap or cooking grease to use. Nor is the Women's Lib stereotype much more appetizing—or coherent—with its high-style ladies (come on, now, girruls, are we really wearing those baubles and beads and eyelashes for the benefit of the other ladies?) wanting to be more equal than anybody on account of they're female.

The day that women will settle for being just people and men come to the same agreement, marriages will indeed be made in heaven. At the moment, they're being made on earth—and, more often than not, by the right people, or so those damned statistics still indicate. And the institution stands firm—at least in the view of this inmate who at this writing has spent half her life on the inside. And as the old doctor at the Grand Hotel used to say . . . *they come and they go . . . and nothing ever happens.*

Born and educated in India, Rustum Roy graduated with bachelor's and master's degrees in chemistry from Patna University, and obtained his Ph.D. from The Pennsylvania State University.

Dr. Roy has been on the faculty of The Pennsylvania State University since 1950 and is now Professor of The Solid State, and Director of the Intercollege, Interdisciplinary Materials Research Laboratory.

He has been involved in initiating experimental community life-styles for students (Koinonia) and for other adults (The Sycamore Community).

Professor Roy has written and spoken widely on these topics and has co-authored, with his wife Della, the widely sold book HONEST SEX!

Rustum Roy

THE INSTITUTION OF MARRIAGE in the form in which it now exists in America is as obsolete as the piston-engined plane in a jet-age. But then, so is the Constitution of the United States. The content of the typical marriage and the U. S. Constitution would both be changed in my ideal remake of the U. S.; yet I know that the change in marriage styles will come long before we fix the Constitution. Since I am not a revolutionary but a scientific radical, I believe that neither institution is about to vanish or to be torn down suddenly. Both these institutions must be supplanted by something more appropriate for our day. The task of the true radical is to work carefully for that new form.

Real changes occur in science when old patterns give way to a more powerful new paradigm which gradually wins more and more adherents. Jets have gradually, but inexorably, replaced piston engines in planes. For the majority of Americans, premarital sexual expression has gradually replaced premarital sexual inhibition. In that sense, I believe that all those concerned with a creative family environment and good interpersonal relations must bend their energies to providing alternate models for traditional marriage as it is now practiced.

I regard marriage—*as now practiced*—to be a harmful institution, unnecessarily and deeply hurting many people, providing unmerited shelter from the growing process of life for many persons. As I see it, conventional marriage for the coming generation is a wholly inadequate governance of the relation between men, women, and children.

The vast majority of my friends are at least mildly shocked at my criticism of the institution of marriage, American-style. I find it amusing, therefore, to hear the same persons raging at the slippery concepts of racist and sexist institutions and whatever the latest scapegoat it is that the *Life-Newsweek*-CBS cartel decrees as the target of the year. Why, then, is the battle against marriage not joined by many more than the "radiclibs"? I believe I have the answer.

First, this conspiracy of silence aims to avoid complexity and tragedy. There are millions of Americans who are, in fact, reasonably happily married; but there are many more millions who would not want it known that they are not. Moreover, the affected don't know many people who are not happily married because most of their friends—like them—are close-mouthed. Few reveal their real feelings about their marriage.

Secondly, there is the bias towards security. There are tens of millions of Americans who, on balance, have a tolerable marriage with all its ups and downs as the textbooks and counselors say; why should they change what they have? Who will guarantee that some other arrangement will prove to be better? Sure, you don't talk about the lousy sex life—since the cooking's not bad. Or why not accede to his bowling games and poker games four nights a week if he buys you a little Porsche?

The insecurity of the median marriage partner about his or her own capacity to do any better at landing a new mate is at the root of the silence which conceals the deeper failures of quality in marriage. It is this insecurity which prevents any concentrated action for change.

Any effective plan for change of the institution cannot appear from within the institution. But, changes occurring at the fringes will affect the major pillars of the structure—the role of children, the place of the working mother, the new sexual patterns. Sooner or later, a new pattern will emerge.

Third, marriage as a social institution is highly dispersed and amorphous. There are no Federal or State Departments of Marriage which can be picketed; few votes are to be gained by a politician's advocating the reform of marriage.

Since I claim that it is traditional American marriage which is obsolete, let us be sure just what that institution is. Traditional American marriage is characterized by the following attributes:

1. Two persons should provide the total intimate companionship for one another. This exclusive relationship should last for a lifetime.

2. There should be no sex outside of marriage, either before or after. "Fidel-

ity" between the partners means no coitus with any person other than the spouse.

3. One's nuclear family has an absolute priority on all demands on one's time, money, affections, and concern—typically, to the neglect of all others.

4. Divorce is always shameful. It announces a failure. It is probably sinful. Divorcing persons should pay a heavy price for the privilege of being let off the hook.

*   *   *

The erosion of the philosophical and religious rootage of our culture has left this institutional fruit—monogamy—stranded high and dry. The content of traditional monogamy was a set of societal arrangements formed by the interaction of the Judaeo-Christian tradition with the evolving demands of society. The much vaunted justification for monogamy, based on its increasing popularity as recorded by the number of licences issued, is as phony as a three dollar bill. The simple fact is that the so-called pair-bonding is mainly an accommodation to the population ratio of males: females in an increasingly egalitarian world society *where no real alternatives have been offered.*

The part that religion plays in forming and sustaining the marriage expectations appears to be misleadingly high and superficial. The Church wields unmerited power and uses opprobrium as the opponent of change. Yet let me demolish once and forever the idea that Western nations frowned on premarital or extra-marital intercourse just because the Church said so. Rubbish! The *interplay* of Judaeo-Christian thought and Western society decided the rules of the game. The most telling arguments in this case are:

1. Jesus, himself, explicitly forbids divorce and remarriage. Yet over the last 150 years, one church body after another has accommodated to that which society first legalized, and now totally accepts.

2. The strictures against premarital sex are very vague in the Bible; this is likewise true of masturbation. Yet, in the latter case, the medical profession used just such vague strictures to bolster its incorrect medical conclusions on the side effects of masturbation, and thus helped to develop the traditional silly position about so-called self-abuse.

Monogamous marriage in a nuclear family[1] can-

---

[1] The family patterns of the early part of the century were much less nuclear, and had the basic character of a "larger family" (the blood-related community). Indeed, even the best of the traditional marriage styles seem to be associated with such strong supra-nuclear family ties.

not be held out by any rational Christian or Jewish theologian as *the* Biblically-based model for the life of the faithful. The fundamental unit of Christian society is NOT—repeat NOT—a "family." "Who is my mother, who are my brothers?" cries Jesus and, disconcertingly for the Mother's Day crowd, replies "Whosoever does the will of my Father."

In another context, He says, "Whosoever does not hate mother or father or brother or sister for My sake is not worthy of Me." It may be true that Jewish society was mainly monogamous during the time of Christ, but neither Jesus nor even Paul makes any reference or claim to this pattern as *the* desirable or only possible pattern.

The family in many eras and especially in contemporary America—that is, since 1920—has been, in the majority of homes, a noxious shield against the reality of Christian community. Only in a minority of homes has the family been what Paul Tournier once called "the school of the person," the seed-bed for developing concerned, loving citizens. In a very real way, the family has been a hot-bed for "egoisme a deux" or "egoisme en famille." The Pauline warnings on the distractions of marriage have proved to be right.

The Catholic Church may well have been right on the importance of celibacy, but the Catholic Church has no other structure to offer for companionship and sex—both of which are much less harmful to total commitment than the demands of a family. With a family in the suburbs, it is just damned difficult to be any kind of a committed Christian. (Pace! pace! you hardy few who make up the exceptions that prove the rule!) For the rule is that the institution of marriage, American-style—*as practiced by the majority*—encourages selfishness, possessiveness, and exclusivity instead of a wide-open sharing and openness. True, the marital contract should be understood to restrict exclusivity to sexuality, but the symbolic damage is done. Our culture says by its ideals: *Marriage is sacred. The deepest interpersonal relationship is an exclusive one! If you share it, you destroy it!*

Is *that* the Biblical message? How does that square with the battle cry of Christian evangelism: share everything for the cause? I say that marriage, American-style, even at its best, runs counter to the religious ideals underlying our culture.

*   *   *

If one now turns to a national grading of the actual performance of marriages, things appear even worse. Marriage, faulted on theoretical grounds, can neither be justified on the grounds of its superior performance as a human institution. Indeed, a sober, simple calculation will show that the unchallenged failures and more hideous outrages committed on persons under the institution of marriage have probably hurt more persons than slavery and segregation. Surely, in 10 to 15 percent of U. S. marriages, women have been treated as property and slaves; add to this number single persons, widows, and divorcées who have suffered as much as any untouchable in India—where at least there is a whole society of untouchables.

What is worse is that no one has spoken out against these outrages. The reader should not misunderstand my point. These criticisms do not suggest that marriage or all forms of institutional arrangements among the sexes should be abolished, anymore than criticism of segregation means that all relations among races should be abolished. Both need changing.

Nearly all experts agree on the dire straits in which U. S. marriage finds itself. Listen to Lederer and Jackson in their book *Mirages of Marriage*:

> *Year after year in the United States, marriage has been discussed in public print and private session with undiminished confusion and increasing pessimism. Calamity always attracts attention, and in the United States the state of marriage is a calamity.*

Vance Packard in his *Sexual Wilderness*:

> *In other words, a marriage made in the United States in the late 1960's has about a 50:50 chance of remaining even nominally intact.*

Clifford Adams concludes from an Identity Research Institute study of 600 couples that while divorce rates show the failure of two out of five marriages, 75% of marriages are a bust. And I would point out that in the last three years alone, the divorce rate has climbed 30%.

*   *   *

The sexual exclusivity concept in marriage is being washed away by the irrepressible tide of the sexual revolution.[2]

Suffice it to list here only the enormous impact of totally uncensored literature, movies, magazines—all of which scream or sell more and better sexuality and sexual experience. None of this material advocates or makes a case for the traditional marital monopoly on sex. In this kind of unequal contest, the traditionalist looks like a weak sister to King Canute trying to stem the tide by exhortation.

Let no one have any illusions. Marriage is at bay because of the change in sexual patterns. Within the last few months, sociologist Peter Berger and Harry Ashmore, President of "The Center for The Study of Democratic Institutions," have pointed to this. The latter states:

> *The most revolutionary thing I see is what's happening to the family due to the change in sexual mores. This is profound. I sus-*

---

[2] See "Is Monogamy Outdated," Rustum and Della Roy *The New Sexual Revolution,* Ed. L. Kirkendall and R. A. Whitehurst, D. W. Brown, N. Y., 1971, pp. 131-148.

pect it produces much of the unrest among the young and accounts for much of the woman's liberation syndrome.

By now, it should have become clear to all that the sexual revolution is unique in the history of revolutions. It is the only one in which within everyone—or at least the vast majority—there lurks a secret sympathizer for the revolutionaries. The drive for variety and quantity of sexual contact is biologically implanted: it may be opposed by other self-interests, but it is there. No other cause—for justice, for liberty, or for women's rights—can claim such a following.

Designers of modified marriage styles should be fully aware of these aspects. The traditional institution was wholly callous about those outside its blessed estate—the single or the widowed. The traditional institution was equally vicious in its provisions for the failures—the divorcing and the divorced.

All systems that deal with human beings—for example, schools and colleges—provide several different outlets or patterns for those with varying ability. Likewise, the system builds in a second chance for those who may fail at the first try, for late bloomers, for dropouts, etc. Not so for marriage. As an institution, it punishes its failures by putting them through the wringer of divorce, mangling human beings already deeply anguished in antiquated machinery, and consigning them to a social twilight.

For the involuntarily single, our society provides

no consolation prize; instead, it provides constant reminders of their misfortune—from the time when they fill out their income tax form to the times when they leave a party alone. The limitations which traditional monogamy places upon the styles, frequency, and nature of interpersonal interaction between persons of opposite sexes not married to each other is wholly incompatible with the demands of contemporary social structures.

* * *

As the satisfaction or fulfillment which a man derives from his remunerative work diminishes, he will turn to other sources of satisfaction. The most important of these is the area of interpersonal relationships. The average American will derive less total satisfaction from "getting on top of his job," "making a million," "climbing the ladder," etc., and more from relating warmly and with feeling to others—to others both of the same sex and of the opposite sex.

Among women, the development is not identical. Here, we will see that the locus of work will be changed from the home and child-rearing to the 9 to 5 world of work. In her case, the reason for developing a vastly expanded network of relationships will be the opportunities presented at work and the adoption of substitutes for her children.

In both cases, American society of the seventies and eighties will present the male and female adult population of the U. S. with both opportunities and desires for enormously increased and varied contacts with persons of the opposite sex. The present limits imposed by traditional concepts of marriage simply are not compatible with such opportunities.

*   *   *

What will the new marriage styles look like? I sketch in the following paragraphs my own judgments about the most probable developments:

The first stage of change will yield pain and anguish in the midst of unguided changeover. The first noticeable development will, in fact, be the gradual appearance of a number of alternative styles—individual experiments really. And because there will be no collective action or major pattern, most of these models are headed for the trash heap of history.

Most of the communes are already contributing their bit to this new pollution. Having studied the movement, convened national gatherings and met with participants of dozens of communes, I feel that while some sort of joint living arrangement will continue on a fairly widespread scale within the college population, the commune as a pattern for life and interpersonal relations is not a live option on the U. S. scene.

This conclusion is based on two very simple facts of life: First, life in a commune demands the mutual commitment, to a substantial degree, of some 10 or more persons. This is a statistically unlikely event. Second, life in a commune demands much more structure and discipline (about authority, economics and sex) than an ordinary marriage; and young Americans today are especially short on discipline. Many communes fail because members cannot agree on who should do the dishes or carry out the garbage.

But the built-in yearning for community, and the innate desire to spend the culture's new-found sexual capital will not be denied. It will express itself in some way or other.

Perhaps, here, as in many other fields, the dedicated amateur will prove to be more helpful than most professionals. Robert H. Rimmer, the novelist, has had and will have, in my opinion, more impact on the lifestyles of the seventies and eighties than any other single American. Bob Rimmer is a solid citizen, Boston businessman in the printing business, and as farsighted as he is careful in his creativity. Rimmer's novels, *The Harrad Experiment, Rebellion of Yale Marratt,* and *Proposition 31* have a single theme: how to expand the family or the intimate community. Each novel conceals within it a meticulously engineered plan on how 3, 4, or 6 people *could* live in new styles of relationship. When I first read these novels, I was impressed with Rimmer's vision and I was intrigued by his ideas. The events of the last two years have provided hints that Rimmer may be onto something profoundly important.

Within the recent past, a most surprising and rising number of persons have come to me and discussed their involvement in such groupings of threes and fours; for example, two couples saying they cannot make it on their own any longer, but have found a way out of their dilemma in a foursome. Young people tell me they are determined never to raise children in a single-couple home. No longer are these straws in the wind, but obvious signals. My intuition, as a physical scientist, suggests that this may be the most probable development for a very simple reason. It is much easier for three or four people to agree on any matter than for larger numbers. Indeed, given an appropriate climate for the equal development of a variety of patterns, it may even prove that foursomes are more stable than twosomes.

I believe that the yearning for community is inborn in us as part of the inexorable evolution of the human species—the social animal placed in an environment of increasingly greater population density. Our recent history in America has warped our consciousness in placing far too high a value on an undefined individual freedom. Hence, we will have to grope our way towards *community* across several generations.

In our groping, I think we will find that the next generation and a few of the over-45s have more to learn from their Judeao-Christian heritage than from empirical sociologists and psychologists. This tradition has always maintained that the fundamental unit of society is the fellowship, the "Koinonia" or community, *not* the nuclear family. Such a community or fellowship might consist of from 2 to 12 persons, who constitute the "significant others" to each other. The group will be bound together by strong primary bonds, similar to those which today bind only twosomes. Somewhat different ties will likely exist between couples, threesomes, or foursomes within the community. Being larger than the nuclear family, this group will be able to reflect back much more adequately to each individual the many different facets of their complex personalities.

Such communities are the basic units needed by today's society. In the next few decades, the characteristics of such communities will emerge through the process of evolutionary selection. There is no hope of guessing as yet at the best patterns. In the meantime, it is the duty of the open society to encourage all responsible attempts to define such community. It is a challenge to individuals to cross boldly into this societal frontier, as did their pioneer forebears who crossed the Atlantic ocean and the Western plains.

Meanwhile, for those who have the determination to move faster, there are a few models emerging. Most fruitful of these in America are the Society of Brothers[3] (Bruderhof) houses and the Ecumenical Institute branches. These are "intentional communities" held together by a purpose beyond their own existence—in most cases, religious. Thoughtful observers of the future would do well to study them to see how they could be adapted for the masses who are now merely destroying the structure of the past, or adapted for the emerging minority turning to Rimmerian solutions.

Monogamy, characterized by an exclusive pair-bond relationship and the minimal nuclear family, will

---

[3] Details may be obtained about these organizations by writing E. I.; 3444 Congress Parkway; Chicago, Ill.; and The Society of Brothers, Rifton, N. Y.

go. It is far from clear what the predominant new pattern will be. What is certain is that there will be a great deal of experimentation, and that there will be the development of a wide variety of life-styles.

Surely all persons concerned for the human condition could agree that much pain and trauma would be avoided if society encouraged—and hence controlled to some extent—these developments by appropriate legislation. New laws should permit polygamy and polyandry and no-fault divorce. Moreover, synagogues and churches should establish the true principles which are central or crucial in a sound marriage of any kind.

Obsolescence of all institutions is as certain as death and taxes. Anarchistic permissiveness, or stubborn resistance to change, calling itself the preservation of values, are the two polarized choices we seem to be offered. The buck finally stops in front of each of us: *How would you like to see the institution of marriage changed to fit the realities of the seventies?* For as President Kennedy said:

> *Those who make peaceful reform impossible render violent revolution inevitable.*

In 1972, Robert R. Bell will be joining the staff at La Trobe University, Melbourne, Australia, as a Visiting Fellow. He is currently Professor of Sociology at Temple University in Philadelphia.

Professor Bell has written more than 30 articles for various professional journals, and is the author of several outstanding books, including SOCIAL DEVIANCE, MARRIAGE AND FAMILY INTERACTION, STUDIES IN MARRIAGE AND FAMILY, and PRE-MARITAL SEX IN A CHANGING SOCIETY.

Robert R. Bell

THE ORIGINS OF MARRIAGE are lost in the dim past of mankind's pre-history. The exact conditions under which this relationship developed can never be known; but over time, certain general patterns that came to be common to most parts of the world developed around the marriage relationship. Marriage became important not only in itself, but also because that relationship became the basic unit upon which the family was generally built. This relationship of the family is explicit in most anthropological definitions of marriage where marriage is seen as a network—simple to complex—of customs and patterns of behavior that develop around a couple who are sexually tied to one another.

Marriage has also traditionally implied some idea of permanency as well as reciprocal rights and obligations between the spouses, obligations to their offspring and to a variety of other relatives. In societies of the past, the husband was responsible for protecting his wife and children from the natural, animal, and human dangers of the environment. One important function of the husband was related to his skills in coping with dangers that his family encountered; this is no longer a relevant function for most males in the United States. The dangers that persons encounter are generally beyond the control of any individual.

Today, police agencies deal with criminal behavior; the medical professions, with dangers to health; and various safety agencies, with environmental threats. Basically, the contemporary male has become unimportant in filling this traditional role.

Marriage has generally implied· that both husband and wife will take on coordinated economic roles. In many societies, it has been assumed that the husband would be the breadwinner as a hunter, or as a warrior, or as a professional, and so forth. It was further believed the wife would assume the role of maintaining the household and caring for the children. In some societies, particularly those that were agricultural, the wife would also work in the fields and be directly involved in the economic functions of the family.

However, in the modern Western world, the economic function assumed by the husband had been performed by him apart from his wife, his children, and his home. This has meant that the wife's roles have all been linked to the family and to the household setting, while that of the husband has been removed from that setting to his place of work. So for most of this century in the United States, the primary role of the husband was as breadwinner and that of his wife as wife-mother.

However, this aspect of marriage has been undergoing significant change. Large numbers of women have also left the home, at least for periods during their adult years, and entered the work force.

Women are increasingly a part of the complex

world around them, and are no longer willing to be manipulated by men. Wives are now living in a much broader world than that of marriage and the family. As a result, an increasing number of women are no longer willing to accept the traditional view that the wife's place is in the home.

In recent decades, there has been a strong trend for society to define women as less economically dependent on husbands, and more and more independent. For example, most states have done away with alimony rights for the divorced woman, for women are assumed to be capable of making their own living.

There is also some indication among young, well-educated couples that the economic role between the husband and wife may be shifted according to need. For example, the husband may work to send his wife to school, or the wife may work to allow her husband to go to school or to remain at home.

In most societies of the past, individuals as such were not important; it was the family that was important. Therefore, in most cultures, marriages were at least in part arranged by the parents; whether or not the couple loved each other was generally irrelevant. Arranged marriages provided for alliances between various families.

But in the United States, with the development of romantic love, mate selection became increasingly the right of the young. This also occurred because families were less concerned with kinship. Individuals increasingly got married for personal reasons, rather than as part of any social arrangement. Today, the functions of the extended families in a marriage relationship are often only ritualistic; the young married couple usually determine the amount of interaction they will have with their extended families. Married couples often no longer live in the same vicinity as their families, and have minimal contact with them.

In the past, marriage was highly important to legitimizing the offspring. Where the extended family was held to be very important, a newborn child who was not a part of a family through the marriage of his mother was seen as suffering a great loss. However, this is of much less concern today. In the Black lower class, illegitimacy is often not considered important. When a large number of the persons one associates with are illegitimate, there is only limited concern with what is not shared by the members of the reference group.

Because the infant has a long period of dependency on others for survival, plus the fact that he must be taught by social beings to become socialized, implies that some persons must take on this function. In almost all societies, this has been the function of the wife-mother. In most societies, the contribution of the father to the socialization of the child has been supplementary, but not absolutely necessary.

It is common to hear the argument that because in almost all societies the woman has been responsible for rearing her children that this is a necessary function of marriage and the family. The fallacy here is that because some pattern has been followed in the past, it necessarily must be followed in the future. This argument ignores the changing nature of society. The wife-mother, as the primary agent of socialization for her children, may even be dysfunctional in today's society. There are societies in which the socialization of children does not revolve around the mother: for example, the Nayara of Malabar, and the kibbutz in Israel.

It has been assumed that two functioning parents are necessary for the successful socialization of a child. This assumption implies that the husband-father and the wife-mother roles reinforce one another. By contrast, the one-parent family has often been presented as an important cause of inadequate socialization. For example, the one-parent family—usually meaning female head—often has been causally linked with delinquency, mental illness, school problems, poverty, etc. When the one-parent home—the broken home—is presented as causally related to personal or social problems, the explanation almost always centers around the missing father. The common argument is that with no father the child has no adult male model, thereby leading to negative effects on the child's socialization. It is also held that with no father present, the mother's role becomes enlarged and distorted because she must perform combined parental functions. The importance attached to the paired-parent family makes it the most socially desirable family form; deviant family types are seen as leading to social or personal problems.

The most commonly assumed need for the pres-

ence of a father in the socialization of a child is that
he serves as a sex-role model. Yet, even in the ideal
family, the involvement of the father is often limited,
and the influence he might have as a sex-role model is
not great.

The stress placed on the great importance of sex-role
models also implies a society where there are important
sex-role differences. There is a good deal of evidence
to suggest that the masculinity-femininity differences,
as expressed in differential roles, are rapidly decreasing.

The decrease in the significance of the father
role has led to an increased importance in the mother
role. But the mother role, too, has been decreasing in
its overall functions—a decrease from a societal peak
that made the role of the mother in American society
a full-time adult occupation, something it has probably never been in any other society. Women in the
United States had been led to believe that being a
mother was filling a career; but this notion was based
on distortion. It did not provide the woman with the
means for adapting to the fact that motherhood really
lasted only about two decades. Many women at-
tempted to continue that role long after it had any
functional worth.

Patterns of child-rearing have changed so rapidly
that mothers often feel frustrated: not whether what
they are doing is right, but whether what they are
doing is still *believed* to be right. In part, the intellectual insecurity of mothers in child-rearing has been met
by child-rearing agencies who claim some expertise.

Thus, there are schools which are now increasingly taking over the care of the young child. There have also emerged more and more specialists who teach children a variety of social skills. In effect, modern society says to the parent that in many areas of child-rearing you are no longer competent.

The wife-mother's giving up of parental functions is also related to the increasing activities for women outside the family setting. Whatever the nature of change, it appears that when the woman gives up in part the socialization of her children, it has not led to any significant problems for the children. Very few studies have found any meaningful differences between the children of working mothers and the children of non-working mothers.

In brief, the reality of the ideal family suggests that today's parents are less involved in the socialization of their children than in the past. The father role is primarily supportive; the functions he performs are minor and replaceable either by the wife or by outside-the-family agencies, without evidence of significant cost to the child. The mother role is comparatively greater than ever when compared to the father role. Many of the traditional functions of parental roles are moving *outside* the family; and the mother is less willing to restrict herself to the wife-mother role.

It is argued that rearing children should not continue to be so demanding on the woman, and that she should have options available through the development of day care centers and other child care agencies. The trend is clear: the function of the mother is to be less demanding and less significant to marriage.

*   *   *

In all definitions of marriage, the sexual bond between the husband and the wife is given major stress. Marriage implies sexual exclusiveness between the partners. Where there has been sexual expression outside of marriage, such rights have only been given to the husband. Almost all societies have been double standard and patriarchal.

All known societies have placed some limitations on extramarital coitus. In most ancient societies and even in most recent civilizations, sexual restrictions *per se* have not been enforced because of morality. Rather, adultery has frequently been seen as a threat to the economic balance of society—more specifically, to the male's property rights.

In the United States, while all sexual relations outside of marriage are morally condemned, the negative views toward extramarital coitus are generally stronger than those directed at premarital sexual intercourse. This is the result of two beliefs: First, in marriage there is an approved sexual partner. Therefore, the individual has the opportunity of having his sexual needs met. Secondly, any extramarital sexual involvement threatens the marriage.

In the past, the American male could often discretely indulge in sexual relations outside of marriage, but under no circumstances was the wife allowed any such sexual outlet. For many Americans, the traditional double standard has been altered to the extent that both partners are expected to restrict their sexual needs to marriage. If the husband has any extramarital rights, then, it is believed, the same rights should exist for the wife.

In the United States, adultery is legally punishable; but actual prosecution is rare; in most states, the penalties are mild. Adultery has had its greatest legal importance as grounds for divorce, since it is the only grounds for divorce recognized by all legal jurisdictions in the United States.

When one examines many cultures, past and present, it is seen that the taboos against extramarital involvement are widespread—although sometimes more honored in the breach than in actual practice. Anthropologists have found that taboos against adultery are common to roughly three-quarters of all societies. In most societies, women have fewer opportunities for extramarital sex. Even where the opportunity exists, there is a lower incidence. But the evidence clearly indicates that if women are given the opportunity for extramarital affairs without strong social and psychological restrictions, many will find extramarital sexual involvement attractive and enjoyable. Generally, in those countries that have made clear progress in the direction of social equality between the sexes, it appears that there is an increased frequency among married women for sexual behavior outside of marriage. This appears to be a pattern for an increasing number of American women—especially among the higher educated.

Why should extramarital sexual behavior have been so strongly controlled? Probably the most important influence has been religion. The only sexual restriction in the Ten Commandments is against adultery. Biblically, adultery referred to an offense against property, and connoted the infringing on the rights of another man. A man did not have to restrict his sexual attentions exclusively to his wife. In fact, if the wife did not bear children, she might present one of her handmaidens to her husband.

There are complex reasons for the breakdown of the traditional morality. Certainly the decreasing influence of religion is significant. But on the broadest level the decrease in control has come about because American society has become urbanized. Our specialized society has developed to the point where the traditional institutions of marriage and the family are of much less significance for survival and physical well-being, and *adultery is no longer a threat to the economy*.

The Kinsey studies have clearly indicated that a large number of husbands and wives find some sexual experience outside of marriage. It cannot be strongly argued that this behavior is frequently attributable to chance circumstances or momentary weakness. While there are no overtly socially approved changes in the attitude toward extramarital coitus, the traditional values no longer exert effective control over the behavior of many husbands and wives. The philandering husband has often had latent social acceptance in the United States, but the philandering wife has not —either in the past or in the present—yet the incidence of the philandering wife is apparently on the increase.

Whenever the behavioral scientist has explained why some people have sexual relationships outside of their marriages, the behavior has been regarded as a sickness. While this may often have been true, it is far from appropriate in explaining why, for many married people, there has been a separation of sexual expression from marriage. For some persons, the activity may reflect a personal hedonistic value. If the moral restrictions are not meaningful, then the individual may take an amoral view toward sex, and enjoy extramarital intimacies.

While most people restrict their sexual expression to marriage, it seems reasonable to predict that this will be less true in the future.

Increasingly, the educated young are having more premarital sexual experiences and feeling less guilty about it. A small number of young couples are experimenting with mate-swapping, an idea based on a single standard of sexual expression for both husband and wife. This approach attempts, at least, to eliminate sexual exclusiveness and jealousy in marriage.

Given the loss or modification of so many of the traditional functions of marriage and the family, what is left? In effect, marriage—*as it was known in the past*—has, to a great extent, disappeared. Yet we will continue to have marriage, but the relationships involved will be drastically different.

Marriage satisfies ego-needs: each of the individuals involved has a close tie to another person, which allows both to give of themselves and to receive from the other. While this arrangement calls for the couple to interact intimately with some frequency, such an interaction does not necessarily depend on the couple's being legally married.

One pattern may be predicted for a number of the young and higher educated:

(1) They will live together for periods of time, and then they may move apart or move into a permanent relationship; in other words, the traditional functions of courtship will overlap with marriage.

(2) The man and woman will establish roles based on equality in their functioning as marriage partners, as parents, and in occupational roles.

(3) There will be less sexual exclusiveness related to marriage. A couple may agree to have sexual experiences outside of marriage, but it will be a mutual decision based on a single standard of sexual rights for both husband and wife.

(4) There will be less permanency in the marriage, with the increasing belief that the couple can terminate their relationship when they both choose to.

Max Lerner, author, teacher and journalist, is currently professor of American Civilization and World Politics at Brandeis University. As a journalist and scholar, he has traveled to almost every part of the world, and has lectured before university groups on six continents.

His newspaper column, which he writes three times a week, appears in the NEW YORK POST, *and is widely syndicated both in the United States and internationally.*

Mr. Lerner has written a dozen books, of which the best known is AMERICA AS A CIVILIZATION. *His most recently published book is* TOCQUEVILLE AND AMERICAN CIVILIZATION.

Max Lerner

If by "marriage" one means a prescriptive monopoly for a tight monogamous union for life—till death or divorce do us part—with all the legalities and conventions observed, then I don't cheer for it, nor do I think it has much chance in the decades ahead.

But if one means something much broader—that makes room for the new emerging forms of the past decade—then I am decidedly *for* marriage.

My guess is that some form of monogamy-cum-divorce-cum-outside-affairs will survive along with other social arrangements, although monogamy will lose the unchallenged dominance it has had.

Obviously, marriage, as we have known it, has been taking a beating. When all the pillars of the temple are being broken in the *agon* of the sexual revolution of the West, it would be strange if marriage remained immune. It hasn't. Nor has the nuclear family stayed immune. Look at the list of challenger movements: communes, group marriage, groupsex ("swinging" or "swapping"), contract marriages (with optional renewals), two-stage marriage (without and with children), Women's Lib, Gay Liberation, the encounter movement, and pair-bond cohabiting, for longer or shorter periods, without benefit of clergy or state.

I don't go along with all these movements, nor

with any of them all the way. Yet in the main, I find them a sign of health, and of a ferment of energies in the civilization. They are very diverse movements. What ties them together is their hunger for a more expressive life, less hemmed in by the Puritan codal restraints. Eros is the common wind that puffs the sails of these movements, and the port they are heading for is greater human fulfillment.

The trouble with much of the pro-and-con discussion of marriage is the either-or feeling that pervades such discussion, as if society had to choose between monogamy exclusively and forever, or the death of monogamy and its replacement by forms of promiscuity. What I see instead is the emergence of new alternatives to add to the old, in a richer mixture of marriage forms than we have ever had in Western history. Like William James, whenever possible I prefer a pluriverse to a monolithic universe. In most of life (I exclude law and the Supreme Court) we practice pluralism and varietism—in work, reading, taste, travel, clothes, religious creeds, languages. Why should there not be a similar pluralism in sexuality, mating, child-rearing, family relations?

At this point some definitions:

By *marriage*, I mean a meeting and mating of true minds and bodies, either in a one-to-one pair or more, with a measure of continuity, with or without legal and religious sanction—although both tend to give marriage more stability.

By *family*, I mean a cluster of people living together characteristically for a sustained period, in a set of relationships growing out of the marriage or marriages, with bonds of everyday linkage in work, play, worship, as well as in bed and board. I have deliberately phrased this in broadly general terms to emphasize the perspective in which the contemporary family movements must be viewed.

Anyone writing about marriage must, in all candor, set down his own bias and values. Mine are for the maximum individual choice that is compatible with social continuity in the area of sexual and affectional relationships and the rearing of children. I believe it is crucial to preserve privacy in this realm, and to minimize the intervention of state and church, while retaining and encouraging religious feeling and sensitivity to community ties.

I am against conformity and uniformity in the deepest human relationships. I care deeply about what happens to the emotional health of children in their growing-up years, when character is being shaped. I also want to preserve naturalness and spontaneity in crucial areas of personality. I care also about what happens to men and women in achieving their human potentials, and maintaining the fullest expressiveness of body and mind and spirit, not just in their youth but in middle and old age as well.

I care about our civilization, which shows signs of coming apart. But while I don't want to add to the disintegrative impulses in it, I have a growing conviction that emotional rigidity and repression may be

worse enemies of the civilization than those newer
relaxations of the old codes which are signs of a re-
newed search for old and lost meanings in life. I find
in this search a freshening impulse which may give a
new strength to the civilization.

*　*　*

The reader may or may not share this credo. Or he
may feel that the credo is good enough, but that the
established marriage forms (in stronger or clearer ob-
servance) are more likely to fulfill it than the newer
ones.

At this point, one must ask whether the breakdown of the traditional marriage and the breakdown
of the sexual codes does not mean that history has
passed a kind of judgment on them, finding them
wanting in the capacity to fulfill human needs.

One may say about the traditional marriage form,
as has been said about Christianity, that it has not
failed: it has not really been tried. But this only points
to the difficulty of its functioning without supports and
without heavy psychic costs. Whatever may have been
true in its earlier phases, the history of marriage in the
industrial age shows greater claims made on marriage,
greater burdens placed on it, a questioning of the
"foreverness" aspect of it, a loosening of the "togetherness" aspect of it, a lessening of the functions
the family performs (a sloughing off of production,
education, even religion), an increasing resort to divorce and to extramarital affairs, and a widespread

sense of alienation.

The most favorable context for the traditional family was in an agricultural society where the husband-father could be patriarch and king, where the woman (sometimes the women, as in the Biblical/ polygamous family) was content with her children and security, and where the extended family formed a genuine community. But since then the family has shrunk and become nuclear; the bonds have weakened; women have asserted their rights; and children, their freedoms.

On the American frontier—all the way from New England to the Pacific—the family still retained most of its original features. In the small new settlements, families made a community available. In America's small towns, even as late as the turn of the century, this was still marginally true, although the dry rot was setting in, and the small town's intolerance became intolerable. In the big cities, everything loosened, much was lost, and little has been replaced. But what was lost was mainly the sense of community.

Historically, the cohesion of the family has been maintained, paradoxically, by three institutions that have been regarded as threats to it: prostitution, divorce, and the extramarital affairs. Prostitution has had a long and honorable history, from the sacred precincts of the Oriental temple to the most recent variations of the call-girl, the B-girl, and the street hustler. Prostitution was meant for lonely men, unmarried or away from home, or for married men who needed something closer to their sexual fantasies. More than anything else, prostitution kept the Victorian family going—as the mistress relation did for the French family and for the Italian family—by furnishing an outlet for repressed sexuality. It is now on the downward arc, mostly because its economics have been undercut by the greater sexual availability of lonely women and girls who want only a "date" and some companionship.

I regard divorce, too, to be not a threat to marriage but a bolstering of it. One out of three marriages in the U. S. is dissolved today by divorce (in California, always a vanguard state, two out of three), and the national rate in the decades ahead will probably become one out of two. But divorce has been misunderstood by the moralists and the preachers and the prophesiers of a Roman decadent doom. It is not a rejection of marriage itself, but only of the existing marriage partner, with a passionate resolve to find a better relationship in another marriage.

The real rate to watch is not that of divorce but those of re-marriage—which has been rising—and the falling divorce rate among the second marriages. The romantic expectations of the first marriage may be continued in the second, but either because of greater knowledge and experience or more mature judgment in mate-choice, the second marriages have a better survival chance. If there is a third or fourth, you get a kind of sequential polygamy.

The extramarital affairs, so difficult in the small

towns and villages of early America, became more possible with the impersonality and mobility of the city. The American "affair" never achieved the patterned and recognized hypocrisy of the French husband-mistress and wife-lover relationship, known to everyone, accepted tacitly, rejected publicly. Nor has it been like the feudal arrangement of master-and-peasant societies, or the slave society of the old South where a planter had an acknowledged wife and children, but also a favored slave-girl and unacknowledged children.

It has been rather a series of furtive and often fleeting affairs (although sometimes also the long-sustained "back-street" affairs), where a middle-aged man caught pleasure when he could with a younger woman, or young husbands and housewives found stealthy satisfactions outside the home with chance pick-ups, or sometimes (as in John Updyke's *Couples*) with partners in their close social set who felt mismatched in their own marriages.

In early Puritan America, these adulteries were branded with the scarlet letter. By the time of Dreiser, they were the common stuff of novels. By Kinsey's time, they had become a staple of American marriage. Today, they have grown even more frequent, serving at once the function of stabilizing some marriages and breaking up others, and often, as the recruiting and training ground of new marriage partners.

✿   ✿   ✿

The growth of the "groupsex" movement in the past decade ("swinging," "mate-swapping," "co-marital sex") may seem, at first sight, to be a further extension of emotional freedom and sexual infidelity. On closer view, it is something very different. This movement is an effort to satisfy the hunger for sexual varietism, so deep in both men and women, without imperiling the marriage intolerably. Husband-wife pairs take a night's holiday, together and yet apart, apart and yet together, swinging and changing partners as in the old frontier square dances, except that the partners are sexual partners. It may be a more or less sedate exchange between two or three pairs for the evening, or a weekend orgy in which an actively sexual woman may take on ten or a dozen mates, including other women in lesbian embraces. But in the end, the clothes are donned again, the good-byes said, and husband and wife return to their workaday existence, perhaps discussing some of the encounters, forgetting others, ready the next time for another mixture which may include some of the old partners, but mostly new ones.

The crux of groupsex (see the vivid narratives by participants in *The Groupsex Tapes*[1]) lies in the dissociation it offers between tender love and sensuality, between varietism and commitment, thus tending to preserve the marriage and family ties while giving the

---

[1] *The Groupsex Tapes*, ed. by H. F. Margolis and P. M. Rubenstein, McKay, 1971

partners a chance to act out their intense fantasy life which would otherwise be repressed, or indulged in with a sneaking sense of guilt.

Gilbert Bartell, a student of the "swinging scene" since 1966[2], is impressed with the "inherent normality" of the swinging married couples he studied, mostly in the Chicago area. "They were average, commonplace, and uncomplicated in almost all respects," he writes. This may, of course, be the midwestern mid-America stamp. Other studies, such as those of Carolyn Symonds in the Los Angeles area, and of James and Lynn Smith in the San Francisco area, show more colorful aspects of personality among the swingers. Further studies may suggest that the differences are less regional than those of class, vocation, and social group. But the central experience of swinging, as most students would agree, was best put by one of the participants, "I have come to learn that sex and love are not necessarily one item and inseparable."

This discovery would not seem so gleaming a revelation if it were not for the extent to which the romantic fantasy has, in the past, dominated the dreams and the expectations of love, marriage, home, and family life. Poetry has celebrated this dichotomy since the *Song of Solomon,* and the notion reached its highest point in the poets of the Romantic movement and the domestic novelists of the Victorian age.

Monogamous marriage contains a considerable

[2] *Group Sex:* Gilbert Bartell, Peter Wyden, 1971

mixture of the fantasy of romantic love, which, in turn, is an expansion of the Tristram-Iseult legend. The emphasis is on four qualities of the love relation: Its *uniqueness* (only these two, none other would be possible for either), its *fatality* (it was destined and inevitable, at whatever cost), its *exclusivity* ("forsaking all others"), and its *invincibility* ("till Death do us part"). Thus you get a blend of sacrament with myth and mystique; but you also get an accompanying fantasy of continuous wedded bliss, both tender and sensual.

What has happened to American marriage is that it has been next to impossible for the reality to keep pace with the myth and the fantasy. What has also happened is that the erotic revolution, reflected and encouraged by the media—by TV, movies, magazines, literature, plays, music, pictures and cartoons of nudes, and even the language of everyday life—has had a striking impact on fantasy and expectation, and on what is considered possible. The women's liberation movement has further galvanized what was already waiting. Without the erotic revolution, the women's liberation revolution would have been impossible. Both the bounds of fantasizing and the claims and expectations for active and varied sexuality have been extended. Some marriages have broken under it, as many psyches have broken.

Groupsex is the way that traditional marriage has found to act out the fantasies and to express the sexual claims and expectations, while maintaining marriage as a going concern. If it is true that at the start of the 70's, several million Americans are taking part in groupsex, my guess would be that double or triple that number will be taking part in it at the end of the decade. It will remain a minority form of marriage, but an increasing minority. In time, it may crowd the majority form—monogamous marriage after premarital co-habiting for a stretch, and with continuing extramarital infidelities and affairs, secret but recognized.

The marriage institution is resilient enough to manage a containment operation in both these instances—the marriage with infidelities and the marriage with intervals of orgiastic promiscuity. Both are rebellions against the Puritan codal inhibitions and prohibitions. But there is a distance between them. The marriage-with-outside-affairs still marks a search for the romantic ideal, and is still experimenting with commitment, seeking the best fusion of love and sex. The marriage-with-groupsex has not only separated love and sexuality, and thus given up on the fusion, it has gone farther: it has settled for some workaday compatibility between husband and wife which usually falls short of love; and it focuses on a partnership in sexual adventures which, to a large extent, holds the marriage together.

In many instances, judging from the interviews, groupsex has been preceded by great difficulties not only in relating to the spouse, but in relating to people in general. If these are average and commonplace people, then a kind of desensitizing and alienation may be more widespread in marriage than we have realized. The paradox about groupsex is that it grows out of both the de-sexing and the depersonalizing of the marriage relationship; yet, in the effort to mend this, it focuses almost wholly on releasing sexual inhibitions, and does this through an added dose of depersonalization. The very people who have difficulty relating turn to an activity in which they can get the outward semblance of relating on a sensual level, without having to relate—in fact, without daring to relate—on a deeper level.

＊　＊　＊

Marriage in communes and group marriage are yet other forms that reach very close to the central malaise of traditional marriage. Commune marriage and group marriage are not necessarily linked; but in the past decade, which has witnessed the cropping up of several thousand communes—most of them short-lived—the linkage of communal experimenting with sexual experimenting has been extensive.

The common drive of all communes is utopian: to find a way of changing society and the world by first effecting an inner change, whether in man's relation to land, or to God, or to property and possessions, or to mating and child-rearing. The compelling purpose is to break away from the socially imposed roles and from the career-lines that have proved to be dust and ashes, and to find freedoms and spontaneity in self-contained communities. As in earlier American communalism, such as we had in the 1840's and the 1850's, the crux of the idea lies in property sharing, in work sharing, and in sexual sharing. And probably the most important of these three is sexual sharing.

What sexual sharing has in common with the other sharings is the feeling that society has moved farther and farther away from the instinctual, that man has been taken away from the soil and from its organic components. So, too, society has also taken man and woman away from tenderness and from true sensuality and from fellow-feeling with others. The aim of the communes has been to overcome the overlaid sexual inhibitions by collective sex; to dynamite the nuclear family and to replace it by an organic extended family; to replace compulsory roles by voluntary and spontaneous roles ("doing your thing"); to find new mating patterns—triads, foursomes, three-couples, group marriage—that will not only add variety and spice to sexuality but will give the children a wider universe of parents, and will broaden and strengthen the basic human connection.

There are aspects of this which strike me as valid; and there are other aspects that are bound to be short-lived because they ignore the human experience in every kind of society over milennia. In trying to get away from technology and to get back to the soil, the communards are now discovering that the soil has its own technology which they must master to survive. In trying to get away from the power structure, the

communards have ignored the need for authority of
some kind. They have foundered on an encounter-
group technique, which though useful in exploring
psychological hang-ups, is not useful in decision-
making. In trying to get rid of the old hang-ups, they
have developed three major hang-ups of their own
which are traditionally resolved in "straight" society:
Who decides what? Who does what work? Who sleeps
with whom?

Because the current crop of communes is so
recent, there have been few studies that are of much
value. *Getting Back Together* by Robert Houriet, 1971,
makes a good start, and presents some vivid day-to-
day details. Pending further knowledge of how they
work out, my guess is that the group marriage aspect
is doomed to failure, exactly because the aim—unlike
groupsex—is *not* to dissociate sexuality from emotional
involvement, and tender love from the sensual em-
brace. The result is a repetition, on another level, of
the kind of rivalries, jealousies, infidelities, and emotional hang-ups from which the communards were
fleeing. *"When me they fly, I am the wings."* [3]

The old Mormon experiments in group marriage,
as well as those of the Oneida Community, had a
longer survival power. They had resolved the authority problem by setting up a patriarchal authority or a
council of elders, in a way that the current communards cannot do, and in a way which also is not

[3] *Brahma:* Ralph Waldo Emerson

very applicable to the marriage problem of today.

But something may come out of the commune experience which will change our marriage system. For one thing, the one-to-one marriage will no longer have a monopoly. In communal living, especially in the urban communes—in college areas and among scientific and professional workers—the triad seems to work out better than other experimental forms. It works best with two women and a man—sometimes in a residential commune which includes in addition one or two couples—in a loose sexual arrangement which seems to have a future. This applies especially to men who need variety and a sense of potency, and to women who are as equally at home with lesbian as they are with heterosexual partners, and who have greater orgasmic needs than a one-to-one marriage can provide. Because the emotional as well as the sexual involvement is truly triangular in such cases, it is less likely to encounter paralyzing jealousies.

Another and more important viable residue is the sense of connection and community that the rural and urban communes have developed, even when they have failed in their efforts at sexual sharing and property sharing. In most cases, the young people—sometimes middle-aged ones as well—who move in together in a city apartment or house, or on a plot of land in Vermont or Colorado or Oregon, are not thinking of making a marriage but of forming a family. It is only later that they may find, almost with an element of surprise, that some form of sexual arrangement has emerged inside the larger group. This is now happening in response to a felt need—the hunger for connection. It applies to many young people who feel unwanted, unneeded, unconnected, coming out of an atomized family situation into an atomized society. The whole encounter-group movement is further evidence of this hunger for sheer human contact, physical and emotional. The encounter groups, reaching many more people than the communes do, may be seen as an effort to carve a larger family relationship out of the formless chaos of the outer world, even for a few fleeting months or years.

I prefer the inclusive family—or if we need another term, a "network" of like-minded people—to the exclusive family: I prefer the organic and extended family to the segregated nuclear one. I feel thus mainly because such an arrangement is likely to work better for psychic health, offer more sexual options, more alternatives for the use of time, cushion the shocks and agonies of mate-relations, get rid of the emotional tightness and restrictiveness. Such an arrangement is also likely to offer an easier growing-up experience for children, with a larger choice of parent figures as well as peer-group figures for comfort and consolation, for tenderness, for identification, and for learning; and is more likely to prepare the children for the more fluid and informal life they will doubtless be living in the coming decades.

*   *   *

The question is, of course, how can you arrive at this kind of inclusive, organic, self-generating community without scrapping the marriage institution which has survived over the centuries and is based on elemental human needs? There are values to be preserved: privacy, tenderness, long-shared experiences with all their reverberations and memories. But there are also terrible psychic scars for husband and wife alike, for children growing up in isolation, or in a jangling jungle of marital warfare, and often not having a strong model with whom to identify. There are desolating lonelinesses and alienations which have become the prime diseases of our time, more killing than cancer or coronaries.

One thing to be said for the various experimental forms is that they offer a freshening breeze in the arid mustiness of institutional forms, a rethinking and remolding of our universe.

For most young people today, the old life-style of college, career, marriage, children, infidelities, divorce, and remarriage is no longer satisfying. Nor do they mean to be caught in the earlier contradictions—that their sexual competence comes years before their career competence, dooming them to a long interval of continence or frustration, and of furtive sexual explorations. The current trend is to live together in a pair-bond, without a marriage certificate or ceremony, with or without children, for as long as the will to stay together remains—and then either to marry formally or to explore another relationship.

This, of course, is not wholly novel: it has been true in the past of the common-law marriages among the lower income groups. What is happening now is a class displacement—cohabiting without legal sanction among the middle-class and the upper-class young, and a greater resort to legal marriage for the lower-class young.

Traditional marriage will survive, but as part of a marriage pluriverse. In the process, the institution of marriage as we know it is bound to be transformed, taking over some elements of the commune, of more widely shared sex, and of the inclusive organic community, in an effort to rediscover the true connection between the human personality and what fulfills it.

The son of a Baptist minister, David Morris earned his M.A. degree in Law at Oxford University.

During World War II, he worked with Quakers in China, then served in the British Army in India from 1944 to 1946. He was a barrister for five years prior to his appointment as Solicitor of the Supreme Court in 1955, a position which he still holds.

His first book, CHINA CHANGED MY MIND, *was published in 1948. His most recent book, published in 1971, is* THE END OF MARRIAGE.

Mr. Morris was married once for 24 years. He has one daughter and one son. Most of his working life has been spent on divorce.

David E. Morris

"THERE IS NO SUBJECT on which more dangerous nonsense is taught and thought than marriage," said George Bernard Shaw in 1908. He then proceeded to devote thirty thousand words to the theme in his Preface to *Getting Married*. He advocated revolutionary changes in the law of divorce.

In the following year, a Royal Commission on Divorce was appointed and three years later completed its examination of the history and law of divorce in England and elsewhere. Its report and evidence totalled approximately one and a half million words. Among the 246 witnesses examined were experts in the laws of the United States. At the time, with the exception of Japan, the United States had the highest divorce rate in the world, namely about one divorce to 12 or 15 marriages. In England, at the same time, less than half of one percent of marriages ended in divorce. One of the questions facing the Royal Commission was whether, if divorce were made more easily available in England, the number of divorces would increase to American proportions.

The majority of the Commissioners said:—

Considering this matter generally, it seems that there are so many factors to be taken

*into consideration in the United States
that it is not possible to argue by analogy
that what may, or is alleged to be, the condition in that country would become so
here, if further facilities for divorce were
granted. It may well be that the increase
in the percentage of divorce in the United
States is due to conditions which do not
apply in this country.*

They went on to say that the unsettling of family
life in the United States was probably due to "facilities
of travel, increase of luxury, a growing spirit of independence, a resentment of restraint as much as to the
operation of the divorce laws."

The minority of the Commissioners who were
against extending the grounds of divorce, and who
included an Archbishop of York who was later to become an Archbishop of Canterbury, took a different
view of the American scene. They wrote:

*One of the strongest reasons for not
allowing desertion and cruelty as good
causes of divorce is the ease with which
they may be utilised for the dissolution
of marriages of which the parties have
simply grown tired, and mutually desire
to make an end . . . experience in the
United States emphatically confirms the*

reality of this danger. . . . The danger lies not merely in the risk of a misuse of law in individual cases, but in the creation of a habit of mind in the people; for there is evidently a tendency in the United States for husbands and wives and their friends in certain classes of society to see no discredit in divorce based on allegations of cruelty or desertion, while judges make no effort to detect collusion but consider it to be their duty to facilitate divorce whenever the parties are obviously tired of one another's society. . . . Those proposals (to extend the grounds of divorce) would lead the nation to a downward incline on which it would be vain to expect to be able to stop halfway.

Prior to 1857, obtaining a divorce in England had only been possible by a Private Act of Parliament, and the procedure was very expensive. There were only two or three such Acts a year. After 1857, it became possible to get a divorce in a court of law . . . a husband only had to prove one act of adultery by his wife; however, a wife had to prove not only adultery by her husband but also some additional ground such as cruelty or desertion. The Victorians took the view that one act of adultery by a wife was something of a character altogether different from even several acts of adultery by a husband; and they did so because they agreed with Dr. Johnson's views of conjugal infidelity:

> *. . . between a man and his wife, a husband's infidelity is nothing. They are connected by children, by fortune, by serious considerations of community. Wise married women don't trouble themselves about infidelity in their husbands.*

The dialogue runs:

Boswell: *To be sure there is a great difference between the offence of infidelity in a man and that of his wife.*

Dr. Johnson: *The difference is boundless. The man imposes no bastards upon his wife.*

Imposing bastards upon the wife of someone else, or of no one, was apparently of no consequence.

Not until 1923 were wives and husbands put on an equality so far as grounds of divorce were concerned. Until 1937, the sole ground was adultery. Between 1937 and 1971, the grounds were extended to include cruelty, desertion for three years, and incurable insanity after five years' confinement.

Since January, 1971, it has been possible to get a

divorce in England, provided the marriage has lasted three years, if:

(a) The respondent has committed adultery and the petitioner finds it intolerable to live with the respondent.

(b) The respondent has behaved in such a way that the petitioner cannot reasonably be expected to live with the respondent.

(c) The respondent has deserted the petitioner for a continuous period of two years.

(d) The parties have lived apart for two years and the respondent consents.

(e) The parties have lived apart for five years, even if the respondent objects.

Under the last heading, a man can desert his middle-aged wife and children, go off and live with another woman, and then force a divorce on his wife, however well she may have behaved as a wife and mother, and however opposed she may be to divorce on religious or other grounds. Women's struggle for equal rights in divorce has left them in this paradoxical position.

Within 18 months of its becoming possible to get a divorce in a court of law, the number of divorces increased from 3 to 300 a year; and the man who was largely responsible for the passing of the 1857 Act, Lord Campbell, wrote:

> *I have been sitting two days in the Divorce Court, and like Frankenstein, I am afraid of the monster I have called into existence . . . there seems some reason to dread that the prophecies of those who opposed the change may be fulfilled by a lamentable multiplication of divorces, and by the corruption of public morals.*

By 1901-5, the average annual number of petitions for divorce and nullity in England and Wales was 812. In 1968, there were 45,036 decrees absolute of divorce and 758 decrees of nullity. The latest legislation (January, 1971) is expected to effect a further rise in the rate per annum. In England, we have already surpassed the United States' rate of one divorce to 12 or 15 marriages referred to by the Royal Commission of 1912, but in divorce, as with so many other things, the current English rate of productivity still lags far behind its American counterpart. So far, we have only reached about one divorce for every 10 marriages, which is feeble in comparison with the United States' present rate of about one divorce for every four marriages.

There can be no doubt, therefore, that in England, as divorce has become more easily available by an extension of the grounds for divorce and an equalisation of the rights of the sexes, there has been a vast increase in the number of divorces. Speaking in the debates in the House of Commons on the 1857 Act one Member of Parliament said:

> *The only consistent conclusion of such a course of legislation was to declare that even the mutual consent of the parties was sufficient to dissolve a marriage.*

The prophets who opposed making divorce easier believed that the number of divorces would increase. They have certainly been proved right; but whether the number of broken marriages has increased is an altogether different and more difficult question to answer. In Victorian England, a large number of marriages of the poorer classes who could not afford the cost of a divorce case were ended by separation orders in Magistrates Courts, or simply by the husband disappearing, often as an emigrant to the United States.

So far as the upper classes were concerned, the last decades of the 19th century provided a series of sensational cases involving prominent members of the aristocracy, a cabinet minister, Parnell, and the Prince of Wales. Unrestricted newspaper reporting ensured that the details reached the largest possible audience whose only rival attraction, in the absence of television, was the pulpit. As the biographers get to work on the eminent Victorians, an increasing number of skeletons is revealed in their marital cupboards. Nor beneath the veneer of middle class Forsythe Saga was marriage, itself, always highly regarded.

Mayhew informs us in his *London Labour and London Poor*, which was first published in 1851, that amongst the London costermongers, at the most only one tenth of the couples living together were married.

> . . . of the rights of legitimate or illegitimate children the costermongers understand nothing, and account it as a mere waste of money and time to go through the ceremony of wedlock when a pair can live together, and be quite as well regarded by their fellows, without it. . . . There is no honour attached to the marriage state, and no shame to concubinage.

Writing of monogamy in 1869, Lecky said:

> It by no means follows that because this should be the dominant type, it should be the only one, or that the interests of society demand that all connections should be forced into the same die. Connections, which were confessedly only for a few years, have always subsisted side by side with permanent marriages. . . . It would

*be, I believe, impossible to prove, by the
light of simple and unassisted reason, that
such connections should be invariably condemned. . . . life long unions should not
be effected simply under the impervious
prompting of a blind appetite.*

No statistics are available, or ever will be, of the
number of marriages which were then, ostensibly, life-
long monogamous unions; but which were, in reality,
empty shells only preserved through the pressure of
religious conviction, social convention, or the wife's
financial dependence. One begins, then, in a complete
fog as to the facts. Is the number of successful monogamous life-long unions less or more than it was in 1850?
Divorce statistics do not and cannot answer the question. The strength or weakness of monogamous
marriage as an institution is much more likely to be
discovered by serious sociological research into people's attitudes to marriage than by lifting up one's
hands in horror at the increased number of divorces.

So far as people's attitudes are concerned, I can
only offer my own limited experience as a divorce
lawyer in England; and my experience is of little value
compared with a widely based survey. In England, so
far, however, marriage does not seem to have become
a very unpopular institution. People whose first marriages fail are often eager to try again. People are
marrying younger than ever. People who have been
unable to get a divorce until the new legislation came

into effect in 1971 are now seeking divorces to enable them to remarry before they die.

On the other hand, there has been over the past few years a public discussion about the whole institution of marriage of which this book is an example and which may have a considerable effect before long.

In England, *Why Marriage?* has been discussed on television under the chairmanship of Malcom Muggeridge. In *The Times*, Arthur Koestler has prophesied that two or three marriages in a lifetime will become normal—"facilitated through divorce by consent." Dr. Helena Wright has recommended that marriage partners should have outside affairs. Other writers have advocated trial group marriages and communal households.

More recently a growing number of women writers have attacked the whole concept of male orientated and dominated monogamous marriage. They feel that the concessions made to the first suffragettes have concealed the fact that, in essentials, the woman's role in the traditional monogamous family has been and still is inferior; that she is primarily treated as a household slave and sex object in a marriage contract which barters the freedom of her soul and mind for the security of her body. One feels that to some of the older married men, this picture of the downtrodden feminine spouse must come as a considerable surprise; and it would certainly have been news to Chaucer's Wife of Bath who favored monogamy on her terms to such an extent that she outlived five husbands and was still eager for the sixth.

Meanwhile, one certain fact in England is the steady decline in church-going and in the respect paid to the Church's traditional teaching of lifelong monogamy. Even as I write, the old argument as to whether or not divorced persons should be allowed to remarry in Church has broken out again in the correspondence columns of *The Times*.

Over the past 18 months, I have noticed amongst some of my younger clients a fundamentally different attitude to marriage as an institution. What is the point, they seem to feel, of going through this curious ceremony? It is becoming much more common to read about and meet couples living together who could—but don't—bother to marry. Indeed, logically, if divorce by consent is allowed by law, it is difficult to see what the object is of the formal marriage ceremony, unless it be to deal with the legal position of children. If marriage serves to regularize the legal status of children, this could be dealt with by legislation which did not invoke a marriage ceremony. It would be quite possible to attach legal responsibilities at the date of birth of a child; and even, if it were felt necessary, to enact that some form of public ceremony should then be gone through.

So far, I have been mainly discussing the question: Is monogamy as an institution on its way out in England? I have expressed the view that in trying to find out the facts, divorce statistics are not the most accurate reflection of the number of successful or unsuccessful monogamous marriages. Still less are they an accurate indication of standards of social morality which, in this context, is so often taken to mean sexual morality.

As an Anglican Bishop said in 1937:

> *If the number of divorces were a safe indictation of social morals it were indeed possible to make the whole community pure at a stroke by prohibiting divorce.*

If the first question is: "*Will monogamous marriage as an institution last?*", then the second question must be: "*If not, does it matter?*".

Clearly, it does matter very much to those who are still influenced by their religious upbringing in the Church's traditional teaching on the subject. But what of the many others? What is to be said for and against monogamous marriage? I hope to learn some of the answers from my fellow contributors to this book.

It is true that I am a divorce lawyer who has been fortunate enough to be happily and monogamously married for 24 years. But how do I know that I would not have been even more happily married if there had been a divorce, and I had married someone else; or had two or more wives at the same time? Only this week I was reading the will of a deceased Chinese gentleman from Singapore who provided after his death for his nine sons, eight daughters, one wife and, to quote his own words, "only three concubines." Might not my wife and children have preferred some other arrangement during the past two decades?

Having been brought up in a civilization which for 2,000 years has been dominated by the views of the Church, we have been conditioned to accept monogamy. We may know from the experience of our own marriage or the marriages of our friends how wonderful a happy monogamous marriage can be, and what hell an unhappy one can be for children, wife and husband; but we have no basis of comparison with any other form of institution.

It is not difficult to compose a formidable list of objections to monogamy—that is, to marriage as a lifelong union of two people. It may have been all very well to seek to impose such an idea on people when the expectation of life was much shorter, and death often proved an escape from a lifelong trap. But do men, nowadays, welcome spare parts transplanted into an old wife? Would they not rather swap for an entirely new model?

If monogamy is praised as the basis of the ideal family, we might recall the words of John Stuart Mill in his book appropriately entitled *On the Subjection of Women:*

> *If the family in its best forms is, as it is often said to be, a school of sympathy, tenderness, and loving forgetfulness of self, it is still oftener, as respects its chief, a school of wilfulness, overbearingness, unbounded selfish indulgence, and a*

> *double-dyed and idealised selfishness, of*
> *which sacrifice itself is only a particular*
> *form: the care for the wife and children*
> *being only care for them as parts of the*
> *man's own interests and belongings, and*
> *their individual happiness being immo-*
> *lated in every shape to his smallest pref-*
> *erences.*

Now an increasing number of women are no longer prepared to accept their former subservient role; and under the influence of the Women's Lib Movement, may be expected to press their claims still further. But each such advance by women imposes more strain on monogamy. An equal partnership is a much more difficult form of relationship to maintain successfully than the old family structure in which father was the boss whose word was law.

So far as sexual appetites are concerned, many men and possibly an increasing number of women appreciate some change in what would otherwise be a monotonous diet.

"Age cannot wither her, nor custom stale her infinite variety" may just possibly have been true of Cleopatra but not of most women (or men); and in any event, Cleopatra would hardly do as the patron saint of monogamy.

There is also a claustrophobic atmosphere about modern monogamous marriage. On the whole, we live in small families with a few children and with no relatives and no servants to broaden the group. At night, we return to our little box houses or our little box flats, shut in like a series of battery hens in an animal factory. Shut in and inbred. Even in its happiness, a small monogamous family is an inward-looking affair, retreating from the pressures of the outside world, seeking a private escape from the public role. As families are encouraged to become even smaller and possibly completely childless, are those inward-looking small family units going to stand the strain of so much togetherness?

Louis MacNeice has put the point much better than I can:

> So they were married—to be the more together—
> And found they were never again so much together,
>> Divided by the morning tea,
>> By the evening paper,
>> By children and tradesmen's bills.
> Waking at times in the night she found assurance
> In his regular breathing but wondered whether
>> It was really worth it . . .[1]

[1] From Les Sylphides: Collected Poems of Louis MacNeice published by Faber & Faber Ltd. of London and Oxford University Press of New York.

What then is to be said for monogamous marriage? If people live longer, they age less quickly. If partnership is more difficult than a male dictatorship, it is more worthwhile.

Writing in 1792, Mary Wollstonecraft said in *A Vindication of the Rights of Woman:*

> *Would men but generously snap our chains, and be content with rational fellowship instead of slavish obedience, they would find us more observant daughters, more affectionate sisters, more faithful wives, more reasonable mothers—in a word, better citizens. We should then love them with true affection, because we should learn to respect ourselves.*

Machinery in the home, controlled contraception, and increased education are giving more and more women the chance to escape from domestic isolation and chores into jobs outside the home.

As for the desire for sexual variety, each couple must choose for itself, just remembering that if the choice is for extramarital variety in sexual partnerships, there is not an increase in experience. There has only been a choice between one form of experience and another. The marriage partners who choose the experience of extramarital affairs may find that they no longer have the experience of such old-fashioned concepts as loyalty and trust.

In the course of my work, I have often encountered husbands who have thought that the experience of variety should be solely a male prerogative and who have been quite shocked to find that their wives feel that what is sauce for the gander should also be sauce for the goose. And even when both husband and wife have been, in theory, in favor of extramarital affairs and taken part in them, they have often not enjoyed the results in practice.

If we were all perfect, it probably would not matter whether we had monogamy or polygamy or polyandry or any other form of institution to govern the relationship between the sexes because our love would cope with the situation. But most of us, I think, need help; and our best chance in this imperfect world is probably to find someone else to love and to be loved by; and by loving and being loved in a family, we may hope to be able to extend our capacity for love outward beyond the immediate family. Our hopes of establishing a loving family atmosphere are more likely to be achieved if we can approach marriage without being too blinded by romantic love. To quote Mary Wollstonecraft again:

> *Personal attachment is a very happy foundation for friendship; yet, when even two virtuous young people marry, it would perhaps be happy if some circumstances*

checked their passion; if the recollection of some prior attachment, or disappointed affection, made it on one side, at least, rather a match founded on esteem..In that case they would look beyond the present moment, and try to render the whole of life respectable, by forming a plan to regulate a friendship which only death ought to dissolve.

The monogamous family has been described by an English playwright as that *Dear Octopus*. Octopus, yes! We have all felt its tentacles entrapping us; we have all felt a desperate urge to escape; but most of us have been lucky enough to know that it is also very dear.

So far I have said very little about the position of children in monogamous marriage, although in my work I am often involved in quarrels between divorced parents over their children, quarrels about where they should go to school, how long they should stay with each parent, whether they should be brought into contact with the other woman or the other man. Each parent alleges that the other spoils the children, bribing them with presents and treats. The children suffer from asthma, eczema, and bed wetting. They lose interest and do badly at school. No one really seems to know whether, if the parents can no longer live with each other on terms of love, affection, and friendship, the children suffer more from a continuation of a loveless marriage or the break-up of the home by divorce. It has, however, been suggested during the past few years that so far as divorce is concerned, a distinction should be drawn between marriages which have children and those which are childless; and that while divorce should be made easily available for childless couples, it should be prohibited for those with children until all the children of the family have reached, say, the age of 16 years.

We may feel we know that where the parents are quarrelling, divorce is better for the children; or we may think that even an unhappy, undivided home is better for them than a complete split. But how does the position of children in a happy monogamous family compare with that of children brought up in differently organized families, or outside any family in communal centers run by the state or by voluntary organizations? Are we entitled to assert confidently that the nuclear family—with wife, husband and perhaps, only two children—is the best method of bringing up children? Are we sure that most parents, who receive remarkably little training in how to bring up children, are endowed naturally with what is required? Is unadulterated mother love, plus a smattering of Spock, good enough, let alone the best method which we can devise? I do not know.

I have a deep instinctive fear of the idea of very young children being taken away from their parents and brought up in a group by others however well-trained in child psychology. And I notice that some of the pioneer child-care organizations are more and more trying to get the children they look after out of an institutional atmosphere and back into families with foster parents. When I think of those various political regimes which have, in this century, deliberately tried to break the family as a social unit by taking the children away from their parents, I regard any such tendency with the deepest suspicion.

In many small monogamous family units, children may be pressurized by a too enveloping maternal love, or be cruelly treated physically and mentally; but the damage which we may cause this way seems nothing to the sinister implications of handing over parental responsibilities to those outside the family.

Writing in 1689 John Seldon said:

> *Of all actions of a man's life, his marriage does least concern other people; yet of all actions of our life, 'tis most meddled with by other people. Marriage is nothing but a civil contract. 'Tis true, 'tis an ordinance of God: so is every other contract; God commands me to keep it when I have made it.*

In *Marriage and Morals,* which was published in 1929, Bertrand Russell boldly advocated that a husband and wife ought to be able to remain good friends in spite of affairs. By 1969, in the second volume of his autobiography, he had modified his views. He said that he did not know what he then thought about the subject of marriage. There seemed, he said, to be insuperable objections to every general theory about it, and he admitted that he was no longer capable of being dogmatic on the subject.

Fools rush in where Russells fear to tread. I do not know whether monogamous marriage will or should last as an institution. It has been described as a third-rate solution to a very difficult problem. So far, I am not convinced that anyone has come up with a better one. I only know that I hope my marriage will last another twenty-four years—but I have been lucky.

Currently Director of the Mental Research Institute, Palo Alto (Calif.), William J. Lederer is perhaps best known as the co-author of THE UGLY AMERICAN *and the author of* A NATION OF SHEEP.

Lederer's educational career was quite dramatic—he was a high school drop-out; enlisted in the Navy; entered Annapolis via competitive examinations; and in 1950 became a Neiman Fellow at Harvard.

During the last few years, he has become interested in what he calls "total functionality of the individual," researching this topic at Esalen Institute (Calif.).

After doing research on marriage for four and a half years, using 278 couples as test cases, Mr. Lederer and Dr. D. D. Jackson wrote THE MIRACLES OF MARRIAGE. *This book is considered by many psychiatrists and psychologists to be the most helpful and realistic work on marriage in print.*

William J. Lederer

IS MARRIAGE obsolete?

It certainly appears so. For every 100 marriages in the United States, there are 44 divorces.

Unfortunately, the marriage process is even in worse condition than divorce numbers indicate. In a survey conducted by Jackson and Lederer,[1] 601 couples were interviewed to determine the general state of marriage. Husbands and wives were interviewed separately and confidentially. On the average, they had been married 8.7 years.

The replies to the first and last questions of the survey provide insight into the condition, the tone, of modern marriage.

The first question was: "Do you love your spouse?"

Only 11 percent of the sampling answered unhesitating, "Yes, I love my spouse."

The next group, consisting of 12 percent of the total, delayed for considerable time, hemmed and hawed, and then said approximately, "Well, let's say we get along better than most."

The largest segment, 43 percent, gave what Dr. Don Jackson called "defensive replies." For example, "I

[1] Made in conjunction with 4½-year study conducted in San Francisco-Palo Alto (Calif.) area and New England area for *The Mirages of Marriage*, by Don D. Jackson and William J. Lederer, W. W. Norton.

don't like Mary because she's mean and vindictive. But I appreciate the fact that she works hard at looking after the kids."

The wife, Mary, said, "Harry and I have lots of arguments. He drives me and the kids crazy. But I can't deny he's a good provider and is generous with what he makes."

Members of this group (the 43 percent), when requested to list what they liked and what they disliked about their spouses, listed more *bad* characteristics than good.

The remaining 34 percent frankly said that their marriages were unsatisfactory.

All the couples—from the "happy" ones down to the outspokenly discontented—were asked the following as the last question: *If you could wave a magic wand which would divorce you and your spouse immediately, without inconvenience, without suffering to anyone in the family, without social censure or expense, would you wave the magic wand and get a divorce?*

Almost three quarters of them answered in the affirmative in some degree.

The survey concluded that over half of all married couples stay together, not because they love each other, but because divorce is too painful, difficult or expensive; and that three quarters of all married couples frequently and seriously think about divorce.

Is marriage obsolete?

Yes, marriage *in its present condition* is obsolete. It has not adapted to the complexities of our modern life. The way marriage functions today, it brings more discord than joy, more negative behavior than positive. We are just becoming aware of this. Sick marriages, like our poisoned air and polluted waters, have contaminated the nation so gradually that until very recently, they have not become a cause for general alarm.

Indeed, for the survival of the individual, even perhaps the race, functional marriage is needed more today than it ever has been in the history of the human species. Today, functional, mutually nourishing marriage may be as necessary to our survival as food, water, sleep, and shelter.

This a strong statement. But there is sound evidence that the health of a community, of a nation, is in direct proportion to the strength and unity of its families.

Our social unrest, crime, and sickness are frequently associated in some way with marital discord and family fragmentation. For example, recent research has shown that juvenile delinquents tend to become more wholesome and law abiding when the discord between their father and mother has been diminished. In other cases, where parental fighting has increased, the juvenile delinquency has also increased.

This principle is not limited to juveniles. It is within the discordant family that crimes of violence are increasing. Ninety-one percent of all homicides committed are violent physical attacks by one member of a family upon another member of the same family. The majority of these homicidal individuals have a history of unhappy childhood and of quarrelling parents.

It is significant that social groups with a low crime rate and a low juvenile delinquency invariably are groups which enjoy functional and happy marriages. Good examples are the Mormons, the Mennonites, the Chinese-American communities, and communities who reside in the rural villages of the midwest. Not only is the social behavior of these groups more harmonious, but they generally claim less sick days per year, and they enjoy a higher financial stability than the more discordant family groups.

Happy, functional marriages have one indisputable characteristic: the spouses have longer-than-average life spans, and their health is more robust than that of the constantly fighting spouses or of unmarried individuals.

General practitioners estimate that about 50 percent of the sicknesses they treat originate because of the debilitating stresses of bad marriages. Dr. Karl Menninger has said:

> *If all marriages were loving, our national*
> *health would improve to the point where*
> *we might have a surplus of physicians.*

No, marriage is not obsolete. But its present structure, customs, and laws are frightfully out-of-date. They were designed for an age when physical survival was the human being's prime interest. Today, in the United States, technology has eliminated most of the old physical hazards. Instead, we have the problem of psychic survival. The wholesome, happy individuals who can cope with the hustle-bustle of today usually come from integrated, loving families. Their home is their small, autonomous universe. Within the home, they are safe and secure. Members of the family are supportive of each other. They give confidence to each other; and thus are able to adapt to fluctuating environments and changing fortunes. No matter what happens, they are able to cope.

If a majority of its citizenry is wholesome and happy, the nation is vital and functional.

The collective American personality indicates a degree of infirmity and disorder. More money is spent on the military (because we are afraid), on civil protection (we are dissatisfied and restless), on alcohol, tobacco, and drugs (we are neurotics) than on all other categories of national expenditure.

Almost every facet of the American personality is moving in the same dark direction. In comparison with other modern nations, our national health is declining. The ecology is worsening so rapidly that it may become a more destructive agent than all foreign enemies combined.

These national trends reflect our individual tendencies. We know we must do something to improve the situation. We must nurture the regrowth of joyful health and a wholesome environment and trust.

How can this be accomplished? Certainly, improvement will not result from laws or any other forms of state coercion. Directives which order people to improve their personal behavior were tried in Germany, in Rome, and in ancient Greece, to name a few places; in every instance, they failed.

It appears that the development of the good life—peace, productiveness, a feeling of usefulness, and love —must come on a personal, voluntary basis.

Functional, collaborative marriage seems to be one of the answers; perhaps the only manner in which citizens, one at a time, can participate and observe the results.

One does not have to be a psychologist to recognize two people who are experiencing a mutually nourishing marriage. Just by looking at them, we know they can surmount almost any hardship, be it physical or psychic. They appear confident, joyful. But the number of these wonderful marriages is small, indeed.

It seems obvious that workable marriages are anything but obsolete! Well, if *workable* marriages are so wholesome and nourishing and if they are required for individual and national survival, then why is marriage currently in such a decadent state? Why has the divorce rate risen to 44 percent? And, if marriage works so well, why would nearly three quarters of all married couples divorce, if they could do so painlessly and cheaply?

Obviously something is wrong; and something has to be changed in the marital set-up. That is what young people feel, even though they do not know specifically what must be done. But the actions of the young make it clear that more and more people are afraid to risk the prevailing miseries of modern marriage. More and more people just simply live together. By using contraceptives, they avoid the responsibilities imposed by children. Children would, such unwed couples believe, force them into legal wedlock, and would diminish their freedom. What is the cause of this frightened, pessimistic attitude?

* * *

Why do marriages go astray?

First: *The wrong people marry each other.*

It is a commonplace that two persons with similar backgrounds are more likely to make a successful marriage than two who have different backgrounds. The more similar their tastes, the less they will have to argue about, the fewer decisions they will have to make; and more energy will be available for positive interaction.

In listening to marital squabbles, I am convinced that "difference in taste" is one of the most difficult hurdles to overcome. A taste difference often is interpreted as *"He thinks he is superior to me."*

A few examples of taste differences are: some people prefer to get up at sunrise, while others prefer to sleep until noon. The early bird usually prefers a big breakfast and a light supper. The late-stayer-upper desires nothing except a cup of coffee for breakfast but wants a fancy big meal at night. Some enjoy opera; others detest opera but dig Dixieland or Rock. Some crave late evenings at smoky, noisy nightclubs; others would rather stay at home and listen to Mozart.

It seems incredible, but spouses, on the average, are not aware of their taste differential during the hectic courting period. The explanation is simple: during courting, each "love mad" individual tries at all times to please the other, even if behavioral fraud is involved.

The courtship falsehoods only can be diminished by long acquaintance. Therefore, the highest probability of a good workable marriage is when a girl marries the boy next door, a boy about her own age, with whom she has grown up and gone to school. The chances of a good marriage are even higher if the two families are in the same occupation or profession, and their ancestors came from the same country.

In such circumstances, the two young people are thoroughly familiar with each other's behavioral repertoire. But most spouses, today, are comparative strangers, even though they believe they have been intimate during their courtship.

As recently as perhaps 1900, husband and wife usually came from the same geographic area. In those days, it was a rare thing for people to travel away from home. Most people were born, were married, and were buried within a hundred mile radius. But today, travel is fast, easy, and cheap. Almost everyone moves. The spouses-to-be frequently come from diverse areas; thus the chances for marriages between dissimilar people have increased—and so has the divorce rate.

According to the Jackson-Lederer survey, approximately three quarters of newly married couples are disappointed and discouraged after about a month of married life. "I did not realize how many compromises I'd have to make. I thought he loved me so much he wouldn't always insist on having *his* way." "If I'd only known what she was really like, I'd never have gotten married."

Second: *People marry for the wrong reasons.*

Most people believe they marry because they are in love. This is not so. Mostly they marry because they are involved in a romance, a physical attraction. They believe the union will "make them feel good." They believe marriage is a magic cure-all which will solve all personal problems and that they will live happily ever after. Individuals in courtship are blinded by "love." Often they sense the disagreeable qualities of the other, but they kid themselves, *"He will change after we get married." "She will change after we get married."*

It wasn't romance which originally stimulated female-male mating. No, cunning Nature took over. The marriage concept first developed in human beings to promote their physical survival and to propagate the race. Gradually, spouses hoped that marriage would bring about an environment where each would enjoy growth and wholesome maturity, and where the dreams of each could be realized. Within such conditions comes love. Love can be defined as an attitude where the security and well-being of the other person is as significant as one's own security and well-being.

If people kept these realistic goals in mind when considering marriage, they would be more careful in selecting mates. If they picked their spouses with the same reason and care as they pick a horse, a car, or a business partner, the chances are the divorce rate would diminish.

Third: *The rituals, customs, and laws of marriage are medieval.*

The paraphernalia of marriage is almost insanely obsolete. The concepts were designed for the medieval family when all members worked together in home industries. Father, mother, children were always in the vicinity of home, collaborating for physical survival. Father usually was in command; and it was a male-dominated society.

Today, starting when the children are about five years old, family members are separated all day, and have widely varied major interests. Because individuals have not adjusted to a rapidly changing world, everyone feels put upon. Father believes he works his head off and gets scant consideration at home. The children protest that their parents are too authoritarian, and that the dictates of their own peer groups should be the dominating factor in their lives.

The wife with young children at home feels she is the one who is "stuck" the most. She feels chained to the home like a slave—usually with no free time in which to study or to enjoy a profession. She also gripes that the expenses for father's business and for the children's schooling and for recreation get precedence over her personal needs. She realizes it is no longer a male-dominated society; but somehow, she does not feel she is being treated like an equal. And she does not know what to do about it.

Yes, the family's needs and patterns have changed, but the customs and laws have not.

The old customs are often useless. Way back in the Dark Ages, they were designed by state and church to increase authority over families.

Today, customs and rituals are oriented to increase business. Indeed, marriage is an $18 billion a year industry, what with caterers, dressmakers, flowers, real estate agents, resort expenses, and so forth.

Everything about the present rituals and customs seems antiquated. For example, bridal showers, bachelor parties, and other endless festivities which come before the wedding usually leaving the bride and groom exhausted. Their wedding night often fizzles. Because of their weariness and tenseness, the bride and groom suffer from a high degree of irritation and bad judgment. They often are unable to adjust to what now has become an involuntary relationship. Eight percent of all brides think of their honeymoon as a traumatic tragedy.

The divorce laws are even more destructive than the out-of-date rituals and customs. Basically, they have not been changed in hundreds of years. Divorce today is so difficult, expensive, and unreasonably painful that the very thought of it often begins wrecking the union during the first few months of marriage. As soon as minor arguments begin, the spouses—usually unconsciously—start jockeying for an advantageous position *in case* a divorce should ultimately happen. Thus, perhaps without knowing it, each provokes the other, so that the other will be the "bad guy" and will be the culpable party if the affair should end up in court.

*　　*　　*

What can be done to bring marriage up to date?

First: The science of "how to pick a marital partner" has to be developed. The old romance method has proved a failure.

In the two years that I worked with university students in the Boston area, I reasoned many of them out of an immediate marriage, and persuaded them to wait for at least one year. In every instance, the couples were happy and grateful. *They wanted someone to tell them to go slow.* They wanted someone to give them a test which would predict the statistical probability of their marriage's being a success. They were glad to hear what the realities of marriage were. Usually, in their hearts they knew the realities; but without outside counselling, the forces and momentum of society tended to overwhelm and push them into careless marriage.

Almost all of the young couples had had sexual experiences; and they were quick to recognize that this is not tantamount to a successful marriage, even if the sex experiences were harmonious and meaningful. They were quick to grasp that marriage is a long-term process; and that if it is a workable one, each partner must reinforce the other.

The young people were glad to go through a long

process of learning how to become familiar with the total behavior of the proposed partner. After having gone through this, they frequently broke their engagement in a friendly manner, realizing that they had chosen hastily and badly.

Second: The science of marital therapy must be improved. With few exceptions, the methods of helping troubled spouses are ineffective. The "cure-rate" is only about 12 percent. Present-day therapy is based largely on the concept that each of the discordant spouses are mentally sick. This is absurd, and the notion frequently results in damaging marriages more than helping them. Marital therapists keep querying the spouses about what is wrong with their marriage, and thus increase the arguments. If one spouse seems to get the upper hand in the therapist's office, the other spends the following week trying to even the score.

Proper marital therapy does not allow much time for negative talk. Instead, it is based on positive reinforcement: *"What do you want the marriage to be?"* *"And what will you do to help it get that way?"*

Therapy cannot be effective with only one spouse. Both wife and husband must be present; preferably, all members of the family.

When I help married couples, I not only insist on seeing everyone, but I also eat with them in their homes, thus observing them in their relationship-environment.

When a therapist permits clients to accuse and harangue each other, the treatment can go on and on—

sometimes for years. Research done by Jackson and Lederer lead to the conclusion that by guiding the spouses into positive behavior, the optimum assistance period is six weeks.

There is very little research being done in the techniques of marital therapy. The National Institute of Mental Health reviewed the contents of professional journals of psychiatry, psychology, and mental health in general; and of the 18,000 extracts, only 26 were concerned with techniques of practical marital therapy.

Psychiatrists and psychologists work hard through many years of intense and difficult training. Little of it concerns the awkward marriage of two mentally healthy individuals. Almost none of it concerns increasing the scope of joyful, functional marriages. These subjects should be added to the training curriculum.

Third: The divorce laws should be changed. There should be "no-fault" divorces. If there is blame, it almost invariably is fifty-fifty. The divorce laws should be based on reality, a reality which realizes that in this speedy, blurred, helter-skelter electronic age people often marry too hastily and carelessly. There will be many mistakes, and the divorce laws should consider them.

The divorce laws should permit either spouse, if there are no children, to file for divorce at any time. One year after filing, if either spouse still wants to split up, the divorce should be granted without penalties to either party. Where children are involved, laws should be amended so as to place the children where they will be best cared for—not assuming "the mother is usually best." Women and men should have equal rights in the divorce courts.

Fourth: Child day-care centers should be built, not only in the community, but also in factories and places of business. This would give young mothers the opportunity to rest, to have some leisure, and to go to work or to school if they so desired.

Hand in hand with the above, spouses should consider the advantages of having children later in life. Usually, the child of parents in their middle thirties is a happier, more stable, more intelligent child than those born of young parents. Also, delay provides the young couple with the opportunity of having real intimacy, to explore each other, before coping with the demands of an infant. As one woman expressed it, "My husband and I want to enjoy each other selfishly while we are young. We want to travel, do things, take chances—things we can't do when we are middle-aged. Have fun now; have babies later."

Fifth: Marital-help centers should be developed in all communities, no matter how small. These should be fun centers, not grim marital hospitals. With proper training—about six months—lay members of the community can do the job. They are quite capable of being marriage guides as long as they stick to the positive behaviors and forbid long discussions of past battles and faults.

Such centers, of course, should have the benefits of a psychologist or psychiatrist. If mental illness is sus-

pected, the individual should be referred to a professional.

Sixth: Women should take steps to make themselves feel as equals in marriage. One way to do this
is for a female born into a middle- or upper-income
background to educate herself into a skill or a profession *before* she marries. Then she will not feel dependent or afraid if she later is alone.

Also, a woman should work until she has a little
money of her own in the bank. This must remain hers
to do with as she pleases. If she wants to "blow" a few
dollars on some frivolity, she should not have to ask her
husband.

For a great many women, acquiring a profession
and some capital seems impossible. About 35 percent
of the U. S. population is so poor and has so little education that acquiring a professional skill which involves
schooling appears to be hopeless. These women work
hard just to get enough money for food. When a women
in this class marries a man who also is unskilled and
has low earning power, the woman is usually trapped
into a life of dull drudgery. Many develop illnesses simply to relieve the frightful monotony of their drab lives.
No matter how difficult it may be, these women should
learn a skill with commercial value.

Seventh: The couple should not be slaves to the
old customs and rituals. They should conduct their married lives in a fashion in which they feel most comfortable. For example, if the wife wants to work in business
and the husband prefers to stay home and look after

the children, that is what they should do.

As long as the spouses nourish each other, comfort each other, reinforce each other, they are helping themselves, their children, and society. By "doing their own thing" the marriage will not hem them in.

"*It requires less energy to enjoy a good marriage than it takes to suffer in a miserable marriage.*" Fighting is fatiguing. Collaborating is mutually nourishing.

*   *   *

Once again: Is marriage obsolete?

Heavens no! But the process and structure of marriage must be brought up to date. The 20th century can be the best of all ages—*if* we utilize the labor-saving devices developed by science. But we must take care not to become enslaved by the technological tempo. We can adjust to today's pace if we but remember to be respectful to, joyful with, and collaborative with our spouses.

Being respectful, joyful, and collaborative with each other is what the good life is all about. That, also, is what the good marriage is all about; and this kind of a blessed relationship will never be obsolete.

A happy and successful wife, mother, and grandmother, Esther Oshiver Fisher has become known as an expert in the field of marriage and divorce counseling.

Her training and experience happily combine work in education, psychology, and law. Dr. Fisher has served on many conferences and boards to improve professional standards for practitioners, and has been instrumental in procuring legislation for the licensing of marriage counselors and psychotherapists.

Her book HELP FOR TODAY'S TROUBLED MARRIAGES *was published in 1968.*

Esther Oshiver Fisher

IF MODERN MARRIAGE be viewed from the perspective of desertion, the activity in the divorce courts, and the bellicose fighting between spouses, marriage does not, indeed, seem worthwhile. Marriage, however, is not to be assessed by its failures, any more than education is to be evaluated only on the basis of dropouts.

There is another side to marriage—the marriage that can be a rewarding, long-term experience. This can be achieved only by those who are ready to commit themselves to a life-long relationship. Such men and women see marriage as an exciting challenge. Though able to walk through life alone, they nevertheless choose to walk together, caring for each other's well-being. They help each other to thrive and to know joy despite the hardships and the pain. Husband and wife feel they are a team—that they are one, and yet that they are two. Each is independent of but not isolated from the other. Each is aware of his own autonomy, but together, they make a team.

Marriage—good marriage—implies commitment. It asks for a love affair with life that rejects despair and self-pity. Marriage demands a love of self which is not narcissistic or destructive to the other partner; rather a self-love that enhances the ability for healthy involvement and concern. Marriage demands respect for the uniqueness of the other partner. Marriage is an investment in time in a human relationship that has the potential for a myriad of rewards.

Yet, I am not a zealot pressing for every marriage to be kept intact, no matter what the cost. As a marriage counselor, my daily professional concern is for the singular psycho-sexual relationship of husband and wife. In my work, I am constantly made aware of the impact of social change upon the marital relationship. More and more, the social, legal, and religious controls on marriage continue to lose their effectiveness. More and more, it becomes necessary to look to the vaguer psychological controls within each husband and wife, if their relationship is to be maintained in a constructive fashion. Despite the difficulties, the sadness, and the struggles that I see, I believe in the validity of marriage.

Marriage as an institution is an imperfect product of man's search for order out of chaos, for perfection in an imperfect world. Marriage stands only as a socio-legal and religious framework which requires constant reinterpretation.

Today's young people, in frenzied search of their "feelings," would throw over all social institutions that stand in their way. One must question the wisdom of negating centuries of experience without having some other proven institutions to take their place. To erase the past totally is to have no future. This does not mean that we should continue all the inequities of the past. It does mean that we should take the best of the past to use as a guide for living in the present.

The question is not whether marriage is valid or not. Rather, the question is: How can the psycho-sexual relationship between man and woman be improved upon within the framework of marriage?

Admittedly, the present rate of divorce is a new phenomenon. When we hear statistics of the increasing divorce rate[1] it would seem that marriage is indeed failing. However, statistics need interpretation; and several factors bear consideration.

Peculiarly enough, despite all the despair over marriage, we live in a very marrying society. There continues to be a notable increase in the number of marriages. In addition, there is a tremendous rate of remarriage among the divorced. With more marriages, there inevitably has to be an increase in the number of bad marriages.

Divorce is becoming more socially acceptable. Yet, among the many divorced I have been known in my research[2] and practice, no one has been for divorce and against marriage. The divorced generally see divorce only as a way out of a bad marriage; marriage is still sought after, and considered to be the ideal relationship one must seek. One need only meet with the divorced in the intimacy of the counseling situation to have deep compassion for the unhappiness, the loneliness, and the depression that is theirs. The gay divorcee and gay blade are myths. If the divorced tend toward much

---

[1] There has been a one-third increase in divorce since 1961, and at that time one divorce was generally stated as taking place for every four marriages made.

sexual activity, they do so out of their profound unhappiness and their desperate need to bridge the gap
between themselves and others. They also mistakenly
believe that sexual activity will prove their femininity
or masculinity. Despite what they have suffered in
marriage, the search for a mate goes on endlessly.

All this is not to say that the concept of marriage
should remain the same as it was. Certainly there has
been, and there continues to be, much quick-change
in our society; and this must, of necessity, have an
impact on the expectations and the goals of men and
women. Years ago, a man married a woman he felt
might be a good cook, a good housekeeper, and a good
mother to his children, while she expected her husband
to be a good provider and a good father. Today, the
expectations are for companionship and love.

Achieving a rewarding level of companionship is
far more difficult for most husbands and wives than
earning a living or being a good cook. Such mutuality
of expectations demands understanding of each other's
deepest values.

In a world where more women are seeking their
own autonomy, and becoming more educated, and are
also working, the character of marriage must change.
Women continue to fight the fight of a despised minority. As women push for their liberation, there is a
tendency for men and women to become more alike
in their behavior. This creates much confusion of roles.

The nuclear family—a phenomenon peculiar to
our technological age—has replaced the extended fam-

ily with its many relatives. The nuclear family has made more demands on marriage than husband, wife, and children can rightfully be expected to fulfill. Mobile, rootless, demanding privacy, and being removed from older generations, this kind of modern family finds only isolation and confusion.

The list of problems affecting marriage is long. It is not very surprising that many husbands and wives cannot make a go of it today. If they have not already determined to divorce, many seek professional help. Consciously they seek help for their distressed marriage; unconsciously, they seek help for themselves. The troubled marriage is only a symptom of personal distress in a distressed and distressful world.

Successful marriage as proposed today is for the more mature, for those who understand the role of time in a relationship, the meaning of commitment, and what it is to give without a guarantee of receiving back in kind. One must know that meaningful, satisfying sex comes as an expression of involvement in a loving relationship.

The immature and the neurotic feel marriage is too difficult. Alienated, unable to love and to give, wanting love on demand, and intolerant of time in a relationship, some are trying various life styles to replace marriage. They search for a solution to their need for an intimate relationship that will fill their emptiness and give meaning to their lives, a fulfillment that they cannot give to themselves or to anyone else. How sad!

They turn to the much publicized communes which

appear to be glorified camps for peer groups without counselors. They create their own kind of extended family. The commune is built upon a horizontal base by which peers relate and satisfy each other's needs emotionally and sexually. The element of time is avoided. Yet humans have a need for the feeling of continuity which can be sensed in the family. The old extended family had a vertical base for relationships that expressed an awareness of time. Notably several generations lived together and were involved with each other exclusive of the intimate psycho-sexual relationship which was left to husband and wife. Can involved peer relationships totally take the place of involved relationships between the generations? And what about the exclusive psycho-sexual relationship between husband and wife that many communes would dilute? Will their men and women ever know the special kind of intimacy of a life time relationship between a man and a woman? Will they who have rejected the past generations see life's meaning, hope, and continuity in their grandchild's face?

Recently, I heard of a group of couples who bought an apartment house and broke down the walls between the apartments. One couple takes the responsibility one week for baby-sitting, another for cooking, etc. Hopefully, they have not broken down the doors of their bedrooms. Yet one can see this arrangement as a potential compromise between the commune and

[2] "Education for the Divorced," E. O. Fisher, unpublished doctoral thesis, Columbia University, 1962.

the nuclear family.

I know couples who live together off the college campus—a kind of playing house with no commitment. At best, the relationship is fleeting. In a sense, there is no difference here between such relationships and those marriages made with the thought that if the marriage does not work out the parties will get a divorce. There is no commitment in such marriages, either.

Nevertheless, there is validity to taking a vow in front of people who are important to the couple. It makes their marriage real to them. They are publicly announcing that they are going to risk something for each other. Someday, when things become difficult between them, the legal-religious framework of marriage will help hold them through the crises, when they have thoughts of wanting out. This can be a maturing experience in itself; and so much the better, if therapeutic help is sought.

Marriage in two stages has been suggested by Margaret Mead. The first stage is INDIVIDUAL MARRIAGE, or cohabitation without commitment. The second stage is PARENTAL MARRIAGE, which entails a ceremony and a commitment to bear and support children. The second stage implies that the couple is ready to make a commitment in regard to children. But what about the commitment to themselves? to their relationship? In any case, what insurance is there against the couple's having undertaken the second stage in good faith, only to find they can't make it?

Something happens with the impact of the wedding ceremony. It seems to activate and crystallize deep unconscious feelings and needs that can become most disturbing to the marital relationship. There is the classic example of two people's living together for years who decide to marry. They have a good sexual relationship, and everything generally is good between them. The night they marry, the husband finds himself impotent.

One man said to me "I have a wonderful relationship with my mistress, why should I spoil a good thing?" Obviously, marriage is a difficult arrangement to which men and women must give much effort. Shall we follow the tenets of those who find it too difficult, and supersede marriage with their experiments and ways of life?

Nevertheless, marital standards are changing. The old-fashioned double standard has long since left us. Until now, the single standard has been that of the male, acceded to by women without too much awareness of their own needs. Women were making demands for equality. Confused and uninformed, they believed equal meant the same. Continuing in the male tradition, they placed heavy emphasis on orgasm, and not enough emphasis on a loving relationship between husband and wife. They demanded that their husbands satisfy them sexually, disregarding their own emotional needs for tender affection. They were doomed to disappointment, for their men now began to measure their virility in terms of their wives' sexual expectations. The husbands' feelings of inadequacy resulted in a tendency to disparage their wives.

With the Women's Liberation movement, the tenor of the single standard is changing. Now women are saying: *Never mind the male standard*—we want our own standard, based on our own needs. The implication is that the single standard be that of the female.

The pendulum seems to be swinging toward the other end. It has yet to come toward the middle where the single standard meets the needs of *both* men and women. When that happens, a man and a woman will be able to develop a companionship in which both will thrive—a relationship where each can accept the reality of the other as a human being, with human limitations.

There are those who might say that such a single standard implies that both the husband and the wife may acceptably have extramarital affairs. A single standard for both does not mean a standard that is destructive to their relationship. Today's marriage asks for a high degree of companionship and vitality in the relationship, which was not expected years ago. If this be so, then anything that drains the vitality of the marital relationship is bad.

Men and women are polygamous by nature. However, hopefully they have learned as they grew to adult state the meaning of being in control of their lives. Before marriage, each should have individually developed his and her own autonomy. If they have not, they are hardly apt to develop their autonomy as a couple.

Autonomy implies judgment and discretion in behavior. If the goal is to keep the marital relationship,
then despite the fantasy and the temptation to have an
affair with someone else, nothing is permitted to intrude
or to hurt that relationship.

In the excessive talk about marriage breaking
down, we tend to lose sight of the validity of a man's
and a woman's wanting to be only with each other—
and for life. Each knows he and she could be with
someone else, but they have something special going
between them. This feeling has to be treated pre-
ciously, with an awareness of what time and timing
can mean in life and in the marital relationship.

Marriage, like life, is a constant ebb and flow, a
coming together and a coming apart. Marriage, like
life, is a day-to-day repetitive process, with occasional
peak moments. When we are young, this concept of
time is hard for us to capture; so we mistakenly think
that if we are to live life fully, we must experience
sustained peak days and nights, rather than moments.
Young people find it difficult to envision completely
the phases of life and the stages in marriage. Each of
these stages creates its own new needs, and its own
demands on husband and wife. The adjustment demands of the early years and the demands of the
middle busy years of rearing a family are different
than the demands of the "empty nest" period when
children have gone their own way, and different again
than the demands of the later stages of married life

and old age, when each spouse needs even more support from the other, as sexual and physical activity
declines, and husband and wife gradually realize that
one of them will someday have to cope with life alone.
If a husband and a wife have developed their own
autonomy, they relate to each other in a constructive,
interdependent way throughout these stages, helping
each to cope with life even better than if he or she
were alone. Such people are not dependent; they are
not leaners, they are helpers.

This description may spell boredom and entrap-
ment to the immature who tend to seek out the new.
A new relationship temporarily assuages feelings of emptiness and isolation, and evokes a thrill that makes one
feel alive. The difficulty is that the feeling is only tem-
porary. The immature know little about the investment
of commitment and responsibility in a life-long relationship that must inevitably be charged with both joy and
sorrow. The immature cannot imagine that a good marital relationship can survive the familiarity of two people's knowing each other for years.

One does not tire of his family if he has learned
to be independent of its members, and can relate to
them in an interdependent fashion. Only when one
leans dependently on his family do things get tough for
both them and for oneself. Like a Rembrandt painting,
a good marriage grows more beautiful as it mellows
with time. There is always something to fascinate and
satisfy the understanding, creative beholder; something
comfortable and good about the familiar. Why does

everything always have to be new? A long-term relationship between husband and wife can yield all the pleasure of a great work of art.

Society tends to place much emphasis on the importance of the biological relationship of parents to children, as though this were the only real parental relationship. The fact is that the validity of the parent-child relationship lies in the attitudes and feelings of the parents toward their children, whether they be the "real parents" or the "adoptive parents." No child flourishes in an atmosphere of rejection and emotional deprivation.

The feelings parents have toward themselves and toward each other are very important to their children. These feelings can be the primary source from which flow the many emotional difficulties which beset children, or these feelings can be the source of the healthy developmental growth of the children. Our children mature earlier today than ever before. They enter the adult world unprepared for the hard work and the commitment that are part of that world. As a result, their marriages and family life are undergoing overwhelming stress. More and more children are emotionally deprived.

The results of life in the Israeli kibbutz have been coming to our attention. With respect to this form of commune, one conjectures whether the Israeli kibbutz produces sounder, healthier human beings. The children are separated early from their parents, reared and educated by professional nursemaids, house-mothers, and teachers. They see their parents daily, but their prime involvement is with their particular group of peers. When they grow to adulthood, they are somewhat alienated from their parents, feel more at home and involved with their own particular group, and make unusually good fighting men—particularly, as has been noted, when they are fighting together with the peers they know.

This is better than no feeling at all, but we really do not know too much yet about the results of kibbutz upbringing. For the emotionally deprived children in our country, such a program might be an answer. Certainly, the better answer still appears to be a constructive loving relationship with parents in a family group.

The commune of the family remains the best structure for the growth of individuals. Relationships between husband and wife, between parents and child, between child and child fuse and criss-cross in a good family to create an on-going maturing experience. In such a family, there is a sense of the exciting challenge of life, the joy of achievement, and a feeling of belonging. The pleasures and ills of one member reach all. Resentment is kept at a minimum.

Understanding and awareness of each other's differences and needs and caring about each other's welfare, together with mutual respect and acceptance form a framework for everyday living. In such family life, anger can be expressed without fear of abandonment, and forgiveness is the order of the day. Though each member is a separate growing person, all are united by ties of blood, love, trust in each other, faith in life, work, shared laughter, shared sorrow and tears, dreams and hopes, memories, triumphs and defeats.

To create and develop a meaningful husband-and-wife relationship which results in a good family is a difficult but wondrous and exciting adventure. This can only be achieved where both husband and wife are in love with and committed to life and to marriage and to each other.

Caroline Bird has long been battling for every woman's right to her own uniqueness as a human being; her right to choose her own life style without being boxed into predefined roles. She has expressed her outrage at sexual stereotyping in her widely read book BORN FEMALE.

Ruggedly individualistic in her thinking, Miss Bird actively takes up the cudgels in defense of her beliefs, whether they be related to women's rights, overpopulation, or the rights of authors. There is nothing orthodox or stereotyped about her, and she is likely to pick and choose her causes even within any area so dear to her heart as Women's Liberation.

Caroline Bird

SINCE WORLD WAR II, most American women have married and had their babies in their early twenties. In 1960, for instance, only 28 percent of the women ranging from 20 to 24 were single. But in 1970, 36 percent of the women in the marrying ages were single.

At graduation, Barbara Ballinger, Barnard '71, was introduced by her friends as the only member of her class who was getting married. The distinction may have been exaggerated; but breakdowns from the 1970 Census available about that time were a surprise even to those who knew that getting married the year of graduation was no longer important to women college students.

The increase was dramatic. Young, unattached women are highly visible. They are a lush market for everything from hair curlers to airline tickets. And since the population grew during the 1960's, the increase in absolute numbers meant that there are now more than twice as many of them running around the country.

Why didn't they marry? Most people—and particularly most men—say, "Why of course, it's the pill. Kids don't have to get married anymore." The reflex explanation is refreshing because it cuts out what my nine-year-old son calls the "gooey stuff," and goes to the heart of the matter: people marry primarily in

order to have sex handy. Logically, they ought to welcome the pill for making available the good thing (sex)
without the inextricable bad thing (marriage). Instead, the whole idea makes mothers and most men
uneasy.

"What's to become of them?" a man-about-town
between marriages asked me rhetorically. "New York
is full of bright, beautiful, expensively dressed young
women. All of them are desperately willing, and some
of them are damn nice girls."

"What's to become of *you*?" I countered. "When
are *you* going to get married again?"

He took the question as evidence of hostility. "Oh,
I'll probably marry again soon enough," he replied,
"I'm tired of entertaining in restaurants. But I'm in
no hurry."

"Well, maybe that's the way the single girls feel,"
I pursued. "New York is full of bright, attractive single
girls. They like men. They like sex. But do they really
want to entertain your business contacts? Do they
really want to get married?"

"Sure say they do!" he retorted.

It's hard for men to grasp the notion that women
may not want to be wives. If a girl is attractive and
single, they figure that she's hung up on sex or men, or
at the best, has had abysmally bad luck. A great many
middle-aged men still believe that women don't get
ahead in business because only the lemons are left to
compete in the business world: the brightest and the
best are removed from the competition to rear babies

in the suburbs. You can even find women who believe this.

The fact of the matter, of course, is the other way around. Single women over 30 are brighter, better-educated, healthier, and happier than single men over 30. Bachelors are worse off than spinsters in every way except salary. Age for age, single men are more apt to be mentally ill, three times as apt to say they are unhappy, four times as apt to say they don't like their work. They are more apt to get sick. They die younger —by their own hand as well as from other causes. And so far as happiness can be measured, they lose out this way. On the Happiness Scale devised by Norman Bradburn of the National Opinion Research Corporation in Chicago, single men score less happy than single women.

The reason is obvious as soon as you think about it a moment. As long as women try to marry men better than themselves, the *best* women (on any scale that matters) will be precisely those who will lose out on the marriage market and enter the career market. There are as many gifted women as gifted men, but the men don't mind—and some even prefer marrying their inferiors; but women are reared to prefer a man they can look up to. The losers in this game are the top women and the bottom men; so inevitably, bachelors are the stupidest, poorest, least competent jerks from the wrong side of the railroad tracks; while the single women, who are frequently derided as "spinsters," are in real life apt to be bright, beautiful, well-born creatures who literally can't find men good enough for themselves.

This is the Marriage Gradient. It has always been around. What is new is that there are now so many exciting alternatives to marriage—alternatives that include sexual relationships—so many alternatives that the brightest women no longer have as much incentive to play dumb. Many more women have been to college; and it doesn't matter that they went just because that's "where the boys are." The mere fact that they have gone to college has raised their aspirations, particularly their aspirations for self-expression.

Talk to the graduates of 1971 and you find them full of unfinished personal business. The best of them are surprisingly unworried about the decline in trainee jobs. "There is so much I want to do," they'll say. "I want to travel. I need to grow up. I want to find myself before I settle down."

Young people of former times postponed serious thought of marriage because they "wanted to have a good time." Now they postpone marriage because they don't think they are ready for it. Marriage sounds too hard. Because they don't have to get married to have sex, young people of the 1970's can be much cooler-headed about the kind of marriage they demand. As the urgency declines, the standards rise to clearly impossible levels.

The new Puritanism demands that the "gooey stuff" be examined not as decoration or lubrication for a relationship—difficult at best—but with the literal eye of a child. In the past, the hypocrisy of the wedding ceremony has been endured with help from corny jokes, and a ritual nervousness on the day itself.

But the brides of the 1970's won't say what they don't mean. These new brides are even rewriting the ceremony. Linda Bird Johnson faced her groom, rather than the minister. Many marry themselves, Quaker style. They read favorite poems, or make up the vows they pledge, or insist on being married in bare feet, or even naked. Parents are sometimes excluded; or the mother, as well as the father of the bride, stands at the altar. It's a way of saying, "Our marriage is not for society. It's for us."

Another expression of the new Puritanism is the refusal to marry a mate on the ground that you can't be sure how you are going to feel about anything next year. Far from being promiscuous, these openly declared "arrangements" are actually conscientious objections to marriage. In practice as well as in theory, the young people of the 1970's are developing a two-step marriage: (1) "living together;" (2) then, if children are desired, legal marriage. Many of the couples who have formalized their marriage after living together for years buy the whole traditional package, including a church wedding and sterling silver.

Young people are waiting to have children, and the demographers studying the abrupt drop in the fertility rate of women 20 to 24 no longer think that the babies will come later. It's not like the Depression of the 30's or World War II, when deeply desired babies

were postponed for practical reasons. Many young
women now frankly say they don't like taking care of
children; or more often, that they simply aren't up to
rearing them, even if adding to the population were
desirable. Increasingly, too, they have "other things"
they want to do.

Are young women staying single because they have
been "corrupted" by Women's Liberation? Maybe. But
I'm inclined to think that the casual relationship is the
other way around. It wasn't until a critical mass of
young women remained single in their twenties that
it was politic to admit out loud that marriage isn't
essential to happiness. Feminism was never deader
than it was during the 1950's, when the marriage rate
hit a new high, and the age of first marriage, a new
low. The ideal of universal, compulsory marriage
boomed marriage counseling—and psychiatric therapy.

A half century ago, when a fifth of our women
never married, marriage itself was psychically unde-
manding for those who entered it. But in midcentury,
marriage became the thing that all but eight percent of
women tried at some time in their lives to do. Everyone
was led to expect a marriage that was a great personal
achievement, like the celebrated love affairs of history.
Everyone was required to improve his sexual performance to virtuosic standards on pain of neurosis. Married
couples expected their marriage to grow; and a marriage that served as a means to any other end was
snubbed as mean-spirited, if not actually immoral.

Rising divorce rates and disillusion with domesticity were the inevitable result; and thoughtful sociologists were beginning to lay the blame not on the frailties of human beings, but on impossible standards for marriage.

"I sometimes wonder where we would be now if the Standard American Marriage had been enforced in the past," Dr. Leslie Koempel, Professor of Sociology at Vassar College, wrote in a popular article "Why Get Married?" Medieval monks, explorers, immigrants, schoolteachers, and women like Florence Nightingale and Clara Barton were necessarily unmarried, she pointed out, as were many of the greatest of our great men.

"The faculty of Princeton once named the 10 biggest contributors to the advancement of human knowledge," Dr. Koempel wrote. "Of the 10, Plato, Newton and Leonardo da Vinci never married; Socrates couldn't make a go of it; Aristotle and Darwin married long after embarking on their work; and domesticity does not seem to have made many demands on Galileo, Shakespeare, Pasteur, or Einstein. Similarly, Michelangelo and Keats never married. Milton, Lincoln, Edgar Allan Poe and Shelley were 'failures' at marriage. How many self-respecting modern American girls would excuse Nobel scientist Irving Langmuir who fell into shoptalk on his way to pick up his wife and walked by her, tipping his hat to her vaguely familiar face?"

The Saturday Evening Post printed Dr. Koempel's views in its St. Valentine's Day issue of 1965 as a "Speaking Out" column devoted to opinions not necessarily shared by the editors, and blurbed the title "Why Get Married?" on the cover, just above a luscious pink heart framing a woman contemplating roses, who was obviously happy to be a sex object. Her answer was obviously that of the management: "For love, of course!"

The media were not, however, hitting young women where they lived, as the rising average age of the readership of major women's magazines attested.

All through the 1960's, each college generation of women differed so radically in its outlook from those in college just before them, that seniors complained that they were as out of touch with the freshmen as with their own parents.

The economic base of traditional marriage was eroding much faster than its ideological base. Men no longer had to marry to get sex. Women no longer had to marry to get financial or even social support. Meanwhile, more young people went to college, remaining single or contracting companionate-style marriages in which the wife was more likely than the husband to bring home the money. As the decade wore on, it was easier and easier for women to get a job of some kind: two-thirds of the *new* jobs created during the decade—13.8 million in all—were jobs employers regarded as "women's jobs." This meant that while more and more women worked—and virtually all young women *had* to work—fewer of them could hope to rise up the promotional ladder. Although nine out of ten women worked at some point in their lives, only one percent ever made the five-figure salaries required to support a family in middle-class, suburban style.

Young women couldn't help feeling gypped. Far from getting it "both ways," as critics of aspiring women have alleged, young women of the early 1960's couldn't get it either way: they couldn't get the good jobs themselves, and they had to work to help support the style of living to which college and television told them they were entitled. In 1970, 41 percent of the wives of professional men—ideal husband timber—were out earning money.

Women's Liberation fell like a spark on this dry tinder. It is probably accidental, but the first women's caucuses withdrew from the Civil Rights Movement in 1968, the year of "the great marriage squeeze," a term coined by Dr. Paul C. Glick of the U. S. Bureau of the Census to describe a statistical wrinkle in the marriage market which demographers warned would make 1968 a bad year for brides.

The "marriage squeeze" arises because the most popular age for women to marry is 20, and the most popular age for men, 22. These ages are now a bit higher. The age gap between the average bride and groom has tended to become less; but the changes are in terms of decimal points per year. The point is that women like to marry men older than themselves. Ordinarily, it doesn't matter, since usually there are as many men of 22 as there are women of 20. But for the women who were 20 years old in 1967, this was not the case.

In 1947, we had a big baby crop. Returning soldiers

settled down and the next year there were a million more babies born than the year before. That meant that little girls born in 1947 had to find husbands from the relatively thin baby crop of 1945.

Thus in 1967, the squeeze was on. It was a year when women of dating age began to complain that "there just aren't any men around," and only the demographers realized that they were speaking the literal truth. Some, of course, married men their own age, speeding the collapse of the age gap between brides and grooms. But since about half the college age young people were in college of some kind, a great many of the girls waited to marry. Many stayed on in college or devoted themselves wholeheartedly to their jobs. The "squeeze" gave many of them a year or two of adult mobility to "find themselves." One way or another, a critical mass of educated young women got a chance to taste the satisfactions of being single and on their own and they were encouraged, if only by "sour grapes," to view the joys of married life more suspiciously than would have been comfortable for them to do as brides.

Women's Liberation did not invent the facts, but it spread them with the explosive force of repressed material surfacing to attention. The fact, long known by sociologists, is that Standard American Marriage is not a good status for women. The case against marriage is getting its day in court. Some of the evidence:

1. HEALTH The health of the married is generally better than that of the single,

but the difference is nowhere near as great for women as for men. Careful breakdowns by age, sex, and marital status suggest that there are many ways in which single women are better off than married women.

This is the surprising finding of a U. S. Public Health Service inquiry into symptoms of psychological distress which was published in August, 1970. The researchers asked a cross section of the population whether they were troubled with nervousness, inertia, insommia, trembling hands, nightmares, perspiring hands, fainting, headaches, dizziness, and heart palpitations.

Contrary to expectations, old maids simply aren't the nervous nellies they're made out to be. Never-married people reported fewer symptoms than the married; never-married white women were strikingly free of nervous symptoms, in spite of the fact that women as a sex were twice as apt to complain as men. It certainly looks as if the institution of matrimony was harder on the nerves of women than men; and the suspicion is confirmed by the further finding that housewives report more psychological symptoms than wives who have jobs. The investigators discerned a new disease, "housewife syndrome."

2. HAPPINESS Studies of mental health made in midtown Manhattan and in New Haven, as well as elsewhere, report the same relationship between mental health and marriage. Married people are better off than single people. They have fewer neurotic symptoms, are less likely to be admitted to mental hospitals, are more likely to score high on the Bradburn "Happiness Scale." But marriage makes a much bigger difference for men than for women; and in some ways, old maids are stabler, less anxious, and "happier" than married women. Married men are happiest, followed at some remove by married women, single women, and single men straggling far behind. Studies of happiness in marriage find that men are more satisfied with their marriages than women.

3. MONEY There's a persistent myth that "women own the country" and that "women have it better because men work to support them." But the myth is usually repeated with a wink or a giggle that indicates the speaker knows he is mythologizing. The fact of the matter, of course,

is that married or single, women never get their hands on as much money at any point in their lives as men do. By last count of the New York Stock Exchange, 49 percent of the shareholders of stock in listed corporations are females, but they own less than 20 percent of the shares, and are less likely than male shareowners to make decisions on buying or selling their holdings, let alone affecting the policies of "their" corporations.

While no one pities rich women, wives of men with capital may have less control over family finances than working-class women who frequently bring in a lion's share of the family income. Clare Boothe Luce is one of the richest widows in America. As the wife of Henry Luce, the publisher of *Time, Life,* and *Fortune,* she has always lived lavishly and been able to buy anything she wishes for herself or her many homes. But she says that the only money that she has really been able to invest in enterprises and causes of her own choosing has been the money she herself earned.

Marriage subjects wives to disabilities as credit risks and candidates for job promotion. A woman lawyer I know who has worked herself up to a senior position with a Federal agency recently married a man who earns less. As a single woman, she had been paying much less rent than she could swing; but as a married woman, landlords refuse to count her income because she is not the "head of the house." When she was a single woman, department stores were delighted to give her credit; but when she went to open an account after her marriage, she found that the store insisted on going by the credit available to her as the wife of a man who was temporarily unemployed. Her long and favorable credit rating as a single woman didn't count.

The most serious disability, of course, is the custom as well as the law which decrees that the "domicile" of a married couple shall be the place in which the husband resides. This means that wives cannot move to new job opportunities as easily as husbands. A wife who seeks a promotion must give information about her family plans that clearly amount to an invasion of privacy.

4. SOCIAL LIFE   Marriage was regarded as insurance against loneliness; and in the regimented life of the 1950's, this was frequently true. Except in the bohemian

quarters of the big cities, parties were given by and for couples, and even bachelors found themselves handicapped by their lack of a party-giving wife. But that advantage is beginning to fade. Even in the 1950's, the ritual round of suburban parties was boring to many of those who participated in them, and was frequently blamed for a rise in alcoholism.

Parties in which men talked shop in one corner of the room while women talked shop in the other corner were the inevitable result of social life based on couples rather than individuals. Young people are sensitive to the sterility of living roles. "I hate to go to a party as half of a pair," one young woman writer complained. "People in Ann Arbor think it's odd, but my husband and I have taken to splitting up social engagements. We go together only when we both want to go."

* * *

If I've made the case against marriage from the point of view of wives, it is only because most people believe with Dorothy Parker that "Men in single state should tarry, while women, I suggest, should marry." But in really egalitarian marriages, husbands can make the same case against marriage as wives. More husbands than is generally realized, for instance, resist transfers that would disemploy their wives.

The fact of the matter, of course, is that the old deal of sex-for-support has long been a dead letter. Marriage is no longer the only way to fulfill any basic human need. It is still the most satisfactory as well as the easiest way to do a great many things, such as rearing children; but it is no longer the *only* way to make a success even of that. The Israeli kibbutz and communal child-rearing experiments in the United States turn out acceptable human products.

Wives can no longer do as good a job of catering, cooking, baking, butchering, nursing, teaching, sewing, child-training or decorating as the specialists their husband's money can buy. Nor can a wife expect to be as good a dancer, hostess, sounding board, business adviser, sexual partner, or showpiece as some women he can find to specialize in one of these feminine roles. So women who are modestly affluent through their own non-bedroom efforts are finding that one man is not necessarily the best partner for chess, sex, camping, partygiving, investing, talking, plumbing, vacationing, gallery-going, and all the other activities which the city offers. *No husband or wife can supply the full satisfaction a single person may derive from a love affair, a sex affair, a job, friends, a psychiatrist, or even, at the end, a top-flight trained nurse.*

Traditionalists who subscribe to the sex-for-support theory assume that marriage will break down if women can support themselves. One sociologist thinks the sex-support deal can be salvaged as long as "working in the bedroom" is easier for women than jobholding. But what happens when sex is divorced from pregnancy, and when women want it as much as men? What happens when sexual intercourse occupies the same role in the life of a woman as it does in the life of a man?

There remains, of course, "love." Love may be grand, but it was never the original purpose for which marriage was intended; and it now has to compensate for a growing list of inequities and inconveniences. At the risk of spoiling St. Valentine's Day, it is relevant to ask exactly what love does for people and whether Standard American Marriage is any more essential to love than it is to sex.

The answer is long; but to put the question is to suggest that love and marriage may not be as inseparable as the horse and carriage of the popular tune. If love is a commitment between persons which provides emotional support, then it is obvious that traditional marriage is not the only institutional framework which can nurture it. If love, mutual support, face-to-face daily relationships are essential or desirable—and I am sure that they are—wouldn't we do better to start from scratch and design an institution specifically to evoke and produce these desirables?

Work groups, play groups, the "gang," the "outfit" in the armed forces, "friends," colonies, collectives, communes—all are doing this work now. Some of these relationships have advantages over traditional marriage. Not the least of these is the frankly experimental and informal character of the group which encourages exploration of the psyche and dispenses with sanctions which shrivel mutuality.

This is not to say that marriage won't survive. The most probable future is going to be the most difficult social situation of all. Many life styles will co-exist. Young people will choose what they prefer, and as they grow, choose again and again. Traditional marriage will satisfy many men and women, but it will never again command the prestige of the "one right way" to live. When traditional marriage is a matter of choice, it will never again confer the security it carried when traditional marriage was the only respectable choice.

Presently a Visiting Professor of Medical Ethics at the University of Virginia and the Robert Treat Paine Professor Emeritus of Harvard's Episcopal Theological School, Joseph Fletcher earned his B.D. from Berkeley Divinity School and his S.T.D. from the University of London.

His professional career has included appointments as Lecturer, Chaplain, Dean, and Professor at numerous colleges throughout the United States and in England.

Professor Fletcher has published more than 100 articles and papers in philosophical, theological sociological, and medical journals. Some of his published books include: MORALS AND MEDICINE, SITUATION ETHICS, MORAL RESPONSIBILITY, *and* HELLO LOVERS.

Joseph Fletcher

FEELING SURGES UP in any talk about marriage. Marriage, after all, is one of the so-called "primary events" in life, and we can't expect people to be neutral. Feelings run strong whether one has succeeded in marriage or failed in it.

Let me be candid, to help the reader correct for any bias that may creep into what follows. My one and only marriage has lasted 44 years. My ideal of marriage is that it will be happy, life-long, faithful, monogamous, and heterosexual. Now, having said this, suppose we turn from my autobiography to the broader question of marriage as an institution. Is it workable? Is it desirable?

The thrust of my answer is going to be something like this: "Maybe it will work, maybe it won't. It always depends on the situation of the individual and of society. And if and when it doesn't work, marriage isn't desirable."

As a starting point, we can acknowledge that the institution of marriage in the Western world is in a parlous state. In the opinion of some, it is actually getting close to terminal illness.

Marriage has always been the legal and contractual basis of the family: a means to an end, not an end in itself. Marriage came about because the family needed safeguards or legal reinforcements of various kinds. Therefore, while the parents of a family are required to be married, the partners to a marriage are not required to have a family. As old Westermarck used to put it, marriage is rooted in family, not family in marriage. If the family is maimed and weakened, then marriage will tend to weaken.

In social organizations as in biological organisms, what doesn't function dies. The loss or atrophy of one vital function after another has pushed the family into a deadly decline.

If we go back far enough into the past, we can see that the family was once the basic economic institution, as in family farms and herds and cottage industries. That *wealth-producing* function has been shifted to other institutions—to the factory, and to the office. The function of *protection*, as it applied during the relatively isolated life of the nomadic and agricultural era, has been transferred to the police and to the military forces of the state. *Status-giving* "station in life" used to be a matter for the family; but in a democratic world of social mobility, that too is a lost family function.

Just as the important needs of income, security from violence, and social status have now withered as family functions, so other functions have seriously diminished: *education* has gone to the school systems; *religious nurture* has been taken over by the churches or disappeared altogether; *recreation* in our urban epoch, in spite of TV and backyard swimming pools, has moved to the schools' extracurricular programs or to commercial suppliers, such as bowling alleys and baseball stadia. Here are six of the family's historic functions transferred entirely or on their way to other institutions: wealth-making, protection, one's place in society, education, religion, fun and games. Looked at coldly and functionally in these contexts, the family has become a liability instead of an asset.

Since it is obvious that some of these functions still remain in some families to some degree, however vestigial, according to statistically determined descriptions on a broad scale, it is important to note that I am speaking sociologically about the functions of a family in the techno-urban West. I am not making universal and unexceptionable statements; nothing of the sort is possible in social analysis. The infinite variety of human interests and preferences, added to the stubbornness of the "cake of custom," provide myriad exceptions. But obviously, family-based economics is backward; family-based defense by the Winchester over the mantel is inadequate, if not actually illegal; family-based education is impossible; Lotto and checkers can't compete with movies and juke bars; and so it goes.

Only one institutional function is still left to the family in a preponderant measure: the *affectional*. Psychophysical intimacies, the dynamics of a personality's life and growth, are still shaped—although as often for ill as for good—in the family matrix.

But is this one remaining function or usefulness—love-making and baby-making—enough to keep the family going, even if the family could keep a monopoly of it—which it can't? Some say yes, some say no. I believe it could be enough, if . . .

But I have to acknowledge that no institution, so radically bereft and pre-empted, so much a victim of use-reduction, has ever managed to hang on in the social process. Recalling the socio-biological analogy, vestigial organs such as the vermiform appendix are dangerous. We can also think of such big and little has-beens as monarchy, midwives, schooners, manorial subsystems, fortified towns, endogamy, crossroads schools and churches, hearth games, magicians, chaperonage, poor houses, royal dynasties, blacksmiths, spinningwheels, and so on.

Urban crowding tends to discourage procreation. Medicine has succeeded, to increase longevity. The dysfunctional family of two spouses and only two children—the zero-population-growth norm of simple replacement—is indeed nuclear, not to say protonic. But the consequence, predictably, will be that as the family's last remaining function—progeny and their nurture—is itself further and further reduced, the reason for familial marriage will likewise be weakened.

Alternatively, we might take seriously the possibility of reviving the primitive longhouse, as in the Soviet creche and the group-care of the kibbutzim, instead of personal home upbringing. Some psychiatric opinion suggests that the close emotions of the nuclear family lead more often to conflict and personality disorder than to constructive good. But such notions are far from verified as yet. In any case, be it well noted that if group rather than nuclear arrangements for the family *do* pass the test, this will only further dysfunction the pair-bond household, and thereby reduce marriage's affectional function.

After all, it isn't sex but reproduction that needs marriage. Reproduction leads to the family structure; and then the family, in its turn, needs marriage. That is the developmental sequence. Therefore, to the extent that we separate baby-making and love-making contraceptively, the family is attenuated. In consequence, marriage suffers a loss of pragmatic sanction.

The number of unmarried adults is growing and will go on growing. We may look ahead, not only to fewer children, but to more marriages without children. Familial marriages will be of shorter duration. And marriages of any kind—familial, romantic, or any combination thereof—more for love-making than baby-making. This kind of analysis cuts some of the ground out from under the Gay Liberation's demand for homosexual marriage. Theirs would be a poor and unfunctional imitation of a somewhat shaky heterosexual institution of the past.

This demotion of marriage may seem like wild futurizing; but it isn't, if by marriage we mean an exclusive sexual partnership of two spouses, especially if we continue, however tacitly, to think with the conventional wisdom and make the assumption that the partnership will be permanent. The following factors must be kept in mind:

1. The hard data on divorce and remarriage ("serial polygamy").

2. The widespread practice of translegal liaisons, acted out by our culture's heroes in movieland.

3. The upsurge of venereal disease and extramarital pregnancies.

4. The disappearance of parietal rules in co-ed colleges.

5. The offering by campus health services of contraceptive medical care to students without regard to sex or marital status.

6. The spread of communes and "group marriage," as well as of trial marriage on the pair-bond plan.

7. The resort to "therapeutic affairs" encouraged by some psychiatrists.

8. Spouse swapping in suburbia.

9. The growth of unlicensed unions between widows and widowers on old age pensions who could not afford to lose "her" pension by getting married.

The "familiar" in the modern era has less and less to do with the historic family; and in consequence, this applies to marriage, too.

We are beginning to hear of a new policy for adopting dependent children by men and women who are single—persons who are either careerists, marriage-scarred, or homosexual, and who simply want children but not marriage. Women ("bachelor mothers") are able medically to have children by artificial insemination from anonymous donors of sperm, or even in some cases, to be implanted with a borrowed and artificially fertilized ovum. They could even hire another woman to gestate and bring their embryos to term for them. And if asexual reproduction—parthenogenesis or virgin births—becomes practicable for humans as it is now for animals, then the male germ cell can be bypassed altogether, making men entirely unnecessary. Some "women's lib" evangelists hail this prospect with joy. In this light, marriage has not only institutional and cultural, but even biological strikes against it—all three. It all adds up to a pretty sobering inventory.

The most common basis of our worry about marriage is the divorce trend, even though that is only symptomatic of the problem. If it continues to be true that one out of four marriages ends in divorce, isn't marriage failing? This state of affairs could never have existed in earlier stages of human society. And for every marriage failure that results in divorce, there is at least another one that should. This makes marriage already a fifty-fifty proposition. The rate of failure will probably continue to rise, whether the divorce rate does or not. Blessed are the successful half.

Alvin Toffler, who foresees radical changes in marriage as a part of our shock from the impending future, nevertheless allows that there are some who "through luck, interpersonal skill and high intelligence will find it possible to make long-lasting monogamous marriage work." [1] But even though the "hominid pair bond" that ethologists and anthropologists talk about goes a long way back on the bio-social line, its *permanent* form has been relatively infrequent and atypical. Almost surely, the only reliable strategy for reducing the divorce rate would be to reduce the marriage rate. The other half are always with us, the unsuccessful half. As human beings we are concerned for them, too. It is ethically absurd to fix one, and only one, model of legitimate love life for all, based upon a system that only works for every other person—or for even fewer than that.

Sentimental people often fail to see that the increase of divorce—which they deplore—is in fact evidence of a genuine commitment to marriage, honestly based on the very sentiment—love—which they applaud. Divorce, especially when it breaks up a growing family, shows that the parties involved put such a high premium on fidelity (sexual monopoly) and on "being in love," that those requirements have become their first-order values, taking precedence over such considerations as the children's needs, the continuity of the home, and any other equities that are being sacrificed. Divorce is a sign of romanticism.

[1] Toffler, Alvin: *Future Shock*. (Random House, 1970)

The classical moral theology of the Judeo-Christian tradition was always family oriented. Marriage was a social contract for the good of society, not merely interpersonal or subjective. In the past, society needed children, more population for more brain and brawn; and for the sake of family stability, eyes were closed to mistresses and visiting jongleurs, as a far better maneuver than divorce and its disruption. Bocaccio's stories, Sheridan's plays, and the Fanny Hill saga are a faithful mirror of pre-romantic mores.

But then, romantic marriage superceded social marriage in the West—although many of the old rites and rhetoric still clung to it. And most importantly, the need of reproduction, other than psychobiological desires, began to shift around, and eventually has reversed. The logical result is that divorce has increased—giving us very reliable evidence, paradoxically, that our commitment to romance in marriage is sincere. The divorce rate runs in direct ratio to the sincerity of our marriage vows. Not sentiment but logic reveals that the more people mean it when they promise both to love their mates and to do so exclusively "until death do us part," the more divorce is apt to follow.

Romance, then, is no friend to family marriage. If romanticism—the longing for an authentic interpersonal love-relationship—persists, while the size and importance of the family declines, then marriages as legal contracts will be built more on sand than on rock. Religious counselors who go along with the new philosophy that the "unitive" side of marriage is as important as the "procreative" side have, I suspect, not caught on to the foreseeable jump in the divorce rate, as people test their marriages by romantic fidelity rather than by "what the kids need."

Either divorces will increase, or marriages will decrease. One or the other. Except for the happy half (or fewer) who can make one union for life do the trick, the outlook is, I think, for changes in the forms that marriage will take.

And, in any case, we can foresee fewer marriages of *any* kind. Sexuality will be deepened and amplified, and sexual partnerships and couplings will increase in number; but marriage as a social contract will tend to change its shape and lose its institutional role-force. The women's liberation movement is by no means causing marriage to try other forms. As a movement, it is primarily a *response* to the objective fact that 43% of our women are in the labor force and that 75% of that number are in full time.

In all likelihood, marriage as we have known it in most of the world in the past—the civilizational past— will have to make way for innovations. Permanent, monogamous, heterosexual marriage will become only one of several variant forms. Our vaunted pluralism, the capacity to accept differences democratically and even to rely upon their creative abrasion and tension within a united society, isn't going to stop short when it comes to sex and marriage. It will engulf them, too.

The *moral* essence of marriage is the relationship, not its contractual forms or institutional patterns. The integrity of this relationship might well be better served—if we stop to think—by some revised versions of savage or pre-civilizational marriage forms.

Suggestions like those of Margaret Mead and Judge Ben Lindsay for trial or student marriage are close in shape to the prenuptial learning practices of most savage peoples, among whom they were precursory to what Mead has called "parental" marriage. In this way, long-established or prefigured forms can become the substance of the most recent proposals.

What is merely novel isn't necessarily good or better. If there is any truth at all in Freud's dictum that "biology is destiny," it follows that since we have postponed marriage and discouraged prolificity, there must be new forms for the expression of sexual maturity. Our cultural lag between puberty and parity is, of course, dangerous, as is the lag between sexuality's emergence and its genital expression; but so is the ostrich strategem of insisting on the permanent model of familial marriage for teen-agers and young adults. It is an absurdity clinically, manifest to marriage counselors and statistically apparent in the unyielding divorce figures.

In this connection, we find still another reason why support for the marital monopoly of sex is weakened. Proposals for two-stage marriage first recommend childless trial or student liaisons of limited duration, and then a parental marriage aimed primarily at the continuity and stability needed to rear children securely. The parental marriage might be with the "student" partner or with another. In the parental stage, it is the children that are most important; they come first, *not* romance. And the logic of this is that extramarital affairs may be given the closed-eye treatment; and that one divorce of a familial marriage would be morally worse than a dozen adulteries—worse by far to break up a family with growing children than to sneak in a little amorous adventure on the side. It was precisely this value order that lay behind the common practice of keeping mistresses, and in the ménage à trois of Christian-Catholic countries. But ethically, the recent posture of the West has been just the reverse—to regard adultery as worse than divorce, as an excuse for divorce.

Whether they follow a pattern of group-sex or are only a federation of pair-bonds, the communes have a very short "half life." But with the growing pressures of urban civilization and the almost impersonal nature of most mass social systems, there may yet be a significant adjustment along this line. People's need for small-scale and personally manageable relationships, such as are provided by the nuclear and the communal family, may find a welcome and corrective compensation for the depersonalizing structures of Toennies' *Gesellschaft* (social system), which pulls us away from the *Gemeinschaft* (community or interpersonal interaction) which we crave. We need to *know* each other, as the sensitivity trainers say; and this is why in the Old Testament "to know" meant to have carnal knowledge of. On the other hand, however, if pair-bond marriages of two partners can't stand up any too well, what hope is there for a communal marriage of six or ten or twenty people? I am inclined to believe that pair-bonds will survive intrusions and accidents better than groups can.

Too much time has been wasted in arguing whether human beings are naturally polygamous, down underneath their social game-rules. It seems to me plain enough that people are very commonly *poly-amorous*—that they want to "make love" with more than one partner. Men have practiced what they want more than women have; but this is only due to the greater freedom of movement that men have enjoyed. This differential is wearing thin as women become more mobile in driving their own cars and working outside the home.

It may be, as some say, that women by nature are not polyamorous; but all such naturalistic reasoning is a snare and a delusion. Very few men or women are truly polygamous; few would be at all inclined to be involved in two or more marriages at the same time. Digamy, perhaps; bigamy, no. A considerable number may even want to avoid any and all marriage; but those who would want two or more marriages *pari passu* are few and far between. And as long as the sex ratio remains roughly fifty-fifty, neither polygynous nor poly-androus marriage is likely to emerge as a pattern for purely pragmatic reasons.

Those who peer at marriage through a rear-vision mirror judge it by the classical model of European orthodoxy. According to this, two people marry for love

when they "find" each other, merge their lives symbi-
otically in a connubial-mutual closeness, and stay together until death does them part. It actually works
out that way for some—as I say, for maybe even as
many as half. But not for the rest, who therefore need
our special compassion. And to assume that it works, or
should work for all "sound" people, leads to a shocking
amount of moralism and perfectionist cant.

Years ago, for example, when I asserted that "unmarried love is morally superior to married unlove"
—an obviously high-order romantic proposition—I was
nearly drowned in a torrent of angry recrimination.
The anger was fiercest among those who are willing to
defend divorce in cases of adultery or "alienation of
affections," as offenses against the romantic principle;
but they do so because, in a contradictory way, they
detest any ethics which put sincere love before the legalism of a marriage license. They are being squeezed
uncomfortably between their romantic principle and
their institutional model.

They cannot have their cake and eat it, too.
Either they are to be coherently romantic—holding
that marriage is validated by authentic love—or they
must be institutionalists—holding that love is justified
or authenticated by marriage. Love in the interpersonal sense is, of course, more than simple sexual attraction. Care and commitment are parts of the
syndrome; these attributes make love genuine and
deepen it beyond just sexual attraction.

When "making love" is by mutual understanding

carried on apart from these romantic factors, it may be justified as a "friendly" human act; but it is not love in any romantic sense of the word. I can recall being asked on a TV quiz show what I thought about "free love." How seriously I was listened to by a studio of teen-age swingers when I answered that there isn't any such thing—that love *always costs something* in convenience and comfort and patience and concern.

Furthermore, the old tag about "by love possessed" holds a profound truth. Love has a fierce possessiveness and exclusiveness. When men and women are "having an affair," it is a sure sign that they are starting to "fall in love" when they begin to resent amorous attentions from others to their partner. It is all very well to say that we *should* be able to express our regard and affection, like the Esquimaux, in the rituals of sex as well as of food and of drink and of shelter, but most people are very far, indeed, from such sexual generosity. Possessive sex relationships run as deep, ethologically speaking, as the dynamics of territorial aggression.

What is in question, then, is not the quality of love itself but its chances of survival if we continue to force it, without any situational grace, into the mold or model we have known in the West for a millennium and a half. Institutions must have some give, if they are to be selectively realistic and meet the judgments of a situational ethics.

The family is no longer so all-important. Baby-making is being subordinated to love-making. With plaudits for begetting only two progeny, the family will take up a shorter span of a woman's life. Sexual maturity and freedom are being reached many years before vocations are won, and before economic independence arrives. Men and women now have a thousand times as many competing and complicating relationships and experiences as they used to have. So married love obviously runs a heavier risk of dilution or conversion.

Nowadays, a woman is a person, not just a Miss or a Mrs. She, too, drives her own car. The overall effect of these new variables can only be that serial or "sequential" polygamy will increase, along with extramarital affairs and satisfaction with singlehood. It is already the case that one out of every four bridegrooms is an ex-husband.

Our biggest mistake at the social-ethical level is trying to routinize, as Weber called it, and standardize marriage on a single invariable model. What we need, if we are to meet human needs, is some variety, some options. Rather than attempting to prop up the mono-model, we should be thinking about how to stabilize different *forms* of marriage. One kind especially needs great consideration: the one in which a growing family is its chief reason for being. Taxes, for example, might be more deliberately and generously tailored to help those with dependents—but of course and by all means, with a firm limit on the *number* of such claimants.

On July 29, 1971, *The Washington Post* reported that Senator Russell Long, in a discussion of the Nixon administration's welfare bill, charged that its provision for AID TO FAMILIES WITH DEPENDENT CHILDREN is "a subsidy on illegitimacy, a cash bonus not to marry" and a form of "corruption." He wanted a rule that if there is "a man in the house," the family should be cut off from help. The moralism and cant here is plain. The obvious limiting principle should be the *number* of such children, but Long paid no attention to that side of it, which affects us all, but only to the "immorality" side of it, which is the beneficiary's private business, not ours.

Toffler futurizes on marriage and comes up with an elective scheme of four kinds of marriages, running by age levels from trial marriage to the family parental kind to career marriage to retirement pair-bonds. Toffler is using the right tool—differential diagnosis— whether or not he gets fully on target. It is certain, at least, that his four-options scheme will not become another mono-model, requiring four stages for every- body. Some will need one; some, none; some, all. There is no need for regimentation. The boiler-plate approach to institutions is everywhere giving way to pluralism. This is what it means to speak meaningfully of freedom and creativity and growth.

Institutional rigidity and monolithic structures, so commonly urged by doctrinaire ideologists, are in for a bad time. Ideologues—theistic or atheistic, humanis- tic or naturalistic—are much too simplistic under the bright lights of choice, variety, and difference. And marriage, which began as a physical union and then became a legal one—to give men property rights in women and their offspring—has now reached the threshold of a *moral* union: a free one, elective to start, and elective to stop.

What lies at the heart of the marriage problem is sexuality. Not just sex or "the sex act," but a whole subtle complex of feelings and attitudes—the sex *drama* —which goes with a person's sexual identity, self-perception, and social image. This complex varies, not only as between the sexes, but as between one individual and another. The combinations and permutations are infinite. In spite of obdurate hang-ups to be expected where sensitive sex-tinged feelings are involved, we have managed to make great progress in sexological investigations and education. I am convinced that because so many of the new generation can "hang loose" about sex, they are far less prurient and far less sex-obsessed than were their more Victorian elders.

As one sample of change, the double standard is, in effect, obsolete. As an injustice, an unethical discrimination, it came about because of the once great ignorance of reproductive biology and the consequent risks of pregnancy, and also because of the property-status of women. Medicine and humanism have now made both of these situations old hat, although we are still in a transitional stage of ignorance and inexperience, as we can see in the present-day figures on pre-marital pregnancies and V.D. Middle-aged middle America has not yet caught on to how their children feel about both the double standard and the marital

monopoly of sex. But signals are being hoisted. Just
the other day, a wealthy friend of mine confided that
"what with the way young women act these days," he
had had his lawyer strike the word *legal* from his will—
"my children and their *legal* offspring"—so that every
child would inherit a share, whether born in or out of
wedlock.

Some say that given this revolution in sex morals,
combined with reductions in the role of marriage and
of the family, there is no future for marriage at all—
at least on the ideal model of permanency. They believe that sameness—when the "fuzz wears off the
peach"—will kill any marriage which has to survive
solely by its romantic merits.

I am sure that this is wrong as a generalization.
Without arguing relative virtues, we can recognize that
while for some the peach gets sour when familiarity
take the place of fuzz, others can be and are—maybe
its true for as many as half of us—quite symbiotic, pre-
ferring over the years the familiar peach to the ephe-
meral fuzz. The sex revolution is a far greater threat
of dysfunction to prostitution than it is to marriage.

To come full circle, then, I would claim that even
though the family has practically lost six of its seven
historic functions, the seventh, love-making and baby-
making, is strong enough to keep the family going; and
that something like half of us will share our familial
marriage with the same partners with whom we share
our youthful sex, our careers, and our old age. The rest
will find that no marriage at all is best; or will find that

one, or two, or three, and even four kinds of liaisons are to be tried. That is a question for decision, not for compulsion. But the *family* marriage will be nuclear as it is now: two spouses and children.

Constancy and intimacy and good faith "through thick and thin" are the highest kind of values for hosts of people, and will continue to be. They may be smart or stupid, modernists or traditionalists, liberals or conservatives—but all alike, they thrive on the riches of full interpersonal commitment and mutual growth.

To repeat what I said to begin with: *"Blessed are the couples in the successful half,"* who marry once and fully, even though "the other half are always with us." In the end, I am sure, the "successful" ones won't help the others if they try to impose an *a priori* monomodel of marriage on everybody, just because these "successful ones" suppose it is somehow the "right" thing.

Gilbert Bartell brings the objective eye of the scientifically trained anthropologist to bear on the capricious tinder box of sex and marriage. Associate Professor of Anthropology at Northern Illinois University, Dr. Bartell has studied and published scholarly reports on sociological patterns in different cultures. His articles include "Apache Suicide Patterns: Affective Magical Acts," "The Yaqui and Mexican Government: Conflict in the Perception of Power" and "Group Sex Among the Mid-Americans."

He is undoubtedly best known to the general reading public in connection with his book GROUP SEX: A SCIENTIST'S EYE-WITNESS REPORT ON THE AMERICAN WAY OF SWINGING. *He has been interviewed about the ideas he expressed in this book on many TV discussion shows.*

Gilbert D. Bartell

WHEN AN ANTHROPOLOGIST is asked to comment on contemporary marriage, he cannot isolate this phenomenon from the culture as a whole. If he is a researcher of the contemporary scene—no matter what culture is being studied—he must bring to commentary a sense of time depth. He brings to his study both horizontal (many cultures) and vertical (historic processes) depth. In short, his primary function is to see a totality of culture, not merely a selected segment as do other social scientists.

Anthropological research is relatively easy in a small-scale culture, a tribe, or a band, but becomes increasingly difficult when one turns his attention to large-scale societies such as the United States. The rapidity of change in certain areas of cultural life within America is striking. Some institutions have shown remarkable resistance to change; while others, such as marriage, appear to be in a ferment of change—even revolutionary change.

Like sociologists, anthropologists define marriage as an institution. But at this point we diverge. Some cultural universals (culture traits shared by all people) have to be spelled out. First, all peoples have some form of family; and second, all cultures have some form of incest taboo. These two cultural universals spell out all that one can say at this level of abstraction.

Marriage, cross culturally, is nothing more than social recognition by the membership of a culture that two or more individuals, not necessarily heterosexual, have entered into a socially sanctioned union. For example, in West Africa a wealthy woman can have herself declared a man, change her name, and marry a woman. The "female father" becomes the new head of a lineage, and she is the socially recognized "father" of children ensuing from any coital liaisons with her wife. In this manner, a woman could become the head and revered ancestor of a patrilineage. It has long been known that the "Berdaches" (transvestites) among the Plains Indians were sought after as wives by male warriors.

Formal structure is not a requisite for marriage. In America, it is one of the myriad means of establishing social sanctioning for a dyadic union. Groups calling themselves, and being called by others, *hippies, communes,* and other subsocieties have their own marriage contracts which do not meet accepted American mores. More important than marriage in meeting social, psychological, and biological requisites is FAMILY.

Some form of family is required, since a human cannot survive the first years of life without aid. This aid does not necessarily come from genetically related humans. The infant becomes socially integrated through inclusion into a family structure. One of the many ways of reinforcing and learning cultural activities (enculturation) is through the socially integrating mechanism of the family. The family is the center for meeting emotional needs. For adults, it regulates the sexual activities of its membership. Sexual activities are ideally confined to culturally defined rules of taboo or incest.

What all this means is that every culture has means of meeting social and sexual requirements through a form of family structure. Cultures have shown a remarkable diversity in meeting these needs. In America, through both custom and law, we have until this time agreed to adopt serial monogamy—a heterosexual union called the nuclear family with divorce permissable but not desirable.

We must turn away at this point from the concept of family to a more important construct of the kin group. As we alluded earlier, the family is only one part of the network of social relationships in a culture. For most societies—particularly those that are pre-industrial—the kin group is the most important element in giving an individual locus in a culture. In effect, this means that the kin group is the unit that maximizes physical and psychological security. Whereas all other men may be your enemy, the kin group offers protection and knowledge based on need, sharing, respect, and reciprocity.

Most small-scale cultures depend on genetic kin groups for this orientation; but as a culture becomes more industrial and large-scale, the genetic kin group may begin to dissolve and change toward a fictive kin group (adopt a non-genetic kin group that acts like a genetic group) such as the co-father system (compadrazco) of Mediterranean origin. This particular system has been detailed most frequently in Latin America, although it is known most popularly in America by the notoriety of the Mafia or the Cosa Nostra. It is, no matter its ultimate activity, a fictive kin group tying its membership together by means of a surrogate family and of mutual reciprocity.

When both real (genetic) and fictive kin groups begin to dissappear, the functions of both can sometimes be replaced by sodalities (voluntary associations) that under some conditions resemble kin structures and their functions. American society has a great number of these: fraternities and sororities, special purpose clubs such as the Masons, the Elks, etc. In some cases, these associations can and do function as a means of relating an individual into a social network that meets social, psychological, and even sexual needs.

If we were to draw a schematic series of relationships through time and space, it would go something like the following: small-scale cultures like the Australian Aborigine or the Eskimo meet survival factors through the extended family band. As cultures become increasingly complex, developing into states and nations which become industrialized, the kin groups based on genetic affiliation begin to dissolve with social and physical mobility, and are replaced by fictive kin groups, and then by sodalities. Although this is not a straight line process, it is operative and has certain implications.

As cultures have evolved, certain elements remain

constant, such as the need of meeting biological requirements of children and adults. There remains the less
obvious need of placing an individual in some known
framework. This may be the most important single
factor—that man is a social animal. As I stated earlier,
man must have a locus. Despite a number of mis-
anthropes and recluses, man's damnable ability to think
symbolically and to try and project his thinking
through language results in his desire—even need—to
transmit his thoughts to others. Thus he is forced by not
only his biological needs, but by his symbolic needs, to
know social relationships and to be integrated into such
relationships.

In contemporary America, the fabric of genetic or
even extended family structure of our agrarian past has
been torn apart. Even the ethnic structure of the cities
in the early 1900's is in a rapid state of dissolution.

The move to the suburbs was an attempt to create
the atmosphere of the agrarian village with isolated
nuclear family units which would foster close family
relatedness. This, too, has failed. A colleague once
joked: "We are all looking for a place to plug in our
umbilical cords."

The concept of community to fulfill the former
functions of the kin group is no longer viable, as we
no longer exist in small rural communities, that at least
ideally, met the fictive kin group function. Even the
urban neighborhood, frequently ethnic, is no longer
extant as urban renewal swings its wrecking ball. The
young people are deserting the suburban cluster, and

rejecting the fictive kin groups of fraternities and sororities, the Elks, and the Masons. Their need for integra-
tion and assimilation has not been met by the large
community and urban sprawl. They have turned to
association through symbolic means—dress, appearance, pop culture, and drugs. All small rewards, as the
associations are symbolic and not real. In short, the ties
that bind meet only the symbolic needs, and not the
need of shared reciprocity. No matter how one identi-
fies through dress or drugs, the membership cannot
turn to others for psychological reinforcement.

Marriage, as related to community and kinship,
does not meet contemporary needs, as it appears to
many to offer the same isolation known by one's
parents. What youth is looking for are viable alternatives.

For many, the isolation of the nuclear family does
meet the needs of our mass-cult image-producing society. Some Americans, feeling their need of increased
sexual activity, are turning toward group sex individually and through clubs. There has been a great deal
of experimenting with group sex; the most prevalent
reason offered by the participants is that group sex is
"recreational." And so within the American idiom,
group sex has blossomed into local clubs and national
clubs. The associated activities—essentially the sexual
exchange of married partners—has produced some interesting results. The majority of the participants have
reported that group sex has enhanced their marriages
on both a sexual and a social level. For although the
activities are sexual to be sure, in a wider sense they

are social, forming fictive kinship ties and a place to relate onself in a mechanistic universe.

As a matter of empirical fact, the divorce rate is significantly lower for group sex participants than it is for the population at large. The majority of the participants are white and middle class. We really doubt that this form of recreational activity will continue in the future, for sexual needs are being met for the younger generation through different means.

One of the many reasons for maintaining the nuclear family, even while experimenting with the loose form of the Tanala Indians joint family, is the rigidity of the legal and the social structures in America. Credit, insurance, renting, home ownership, schooling: these all favor—in fact, promote—the maintainence of the legal nuclear family.

We have no cultural tradition for the commune, although it has worked in Israel where it has positive social sanction. It may well be an ideal situation, but it has little chance to survive in America. As communes are now constituted, they are composed of autonomous individuals grouped together looking for a sense of kinship community. The commune can survive if real kinship reciprocity evolves. There is, however, no cultural pattern as yet for communes in America. The Kibbutz survives, not only because it was conceived as an ideal, but because it is under physical attack and threatened by outsiders. Furthermore, as children are born and reared in the Kibbutz, they begin to feel the reality of family-like relationships. When this happens in America, the commune will be viable.

One thing apparent is that the nuclear family does not meet the needs of contemporary men and women. It has not become a place of refuge and of trust. As they become further removed from the integrative nature of the society, men and women require a sense of belonging to a larger community. It is well and good to imagine that one can relate to a whole city, a New York or a Chicago, or to a State, or to a Nation. Man is still not ready for that. His personal needs cannot really be met by a New York. Yet as his world consciousness expands, it is doubtful whether these personal needs can be fully met within the nuclear family. Nor will they be met with serial monogamy. There is a constant change through divorce and remarriage. Each time, the same situation of dyadic heterosexual or homosexual unions is recreated.

There is little fear that children will be abandoned. Individuals, no matter their rationale, will continue to be compassionate and care for and maintain children. Children and adults need a place to belong; and though it is important to have a center of attachment, it by no means follows that this center must be one's biological parents, or that it be restricted to two people, one man and one woman.

In the same light, it is not too absurd to say that one man and one woman may continue to desire to maintain a dyadic relationship with or without legal marriage. These unions can and will continue, as they, too, meet needs of familiarity, knowledge, and trust.

They may exist simply because they are comfortable, and because they offer an oasis of habit where one does not have to work too hard at establishing or maintaining relationships.

Finally, seen from the vantage point of anthropology, men in the contemporary American society are desperately in need of kinship or community. Contemporary marriage is not sufficient to meet all one's needs. We see the best hope for those needing this form of community in loose agregates of people with or without legal sanctions.

We have known for a long time of polyandry (plural male spouses) and polygamy (plural female spouses) and of the ménage à trois. In the first two, the unions become sanctioned marriage patterns within a culture, while the ménage à trois was usually restricted to an elitist group. What we do see developing in America are triads—sometimes two females and one male, or two males and one female—and quadrads. These extra-legal combinations are ideally formed as reciprocal love relationships, sometimes (but not always) including both heterosexual and bisexual (ambisexual) relationships. Although these socio-sexual groupings may not be of long-term duration, they offer a viable alternative to dyads, loneliness, or the unwieldy conditions of a commune.

The relationships offer a number of advantages: extension of sexual gratification; shared emotional needs with more than one person; reinforcement and ego building by a close kin-like group; and an end to loneliness. The definite advantage of the triads and the quadrads over the commune is that the latter, simply due to size, does not offer as personalized a face-to-face resolution of the daily problems of living together.

Furthermore, in urban areas where there are unequal numbers of males or of females, these new forms can offer the previously mentioned reinforcements. Triads or quadrads may, therefore, help to extend psychological and social needs, as well as sexual needs. One need not be quite so fearful of the loss of one person for emotional gratification, since one can easily substitute another member of the group. Within these groups, shared ownership of buildings and of responsibilities also coincides with American codes.

Contemporary changes have thus made obsolete the marriage model based on our agrarian past. I do not mean to imply that marriage is doomed. What I do hope is that varieties of union will be permitted and not be outlawed. My own position is that we should change our thinking by considering larger extensions of the family, rather than a continuation of the isolated and vulnerable nuclear family.

After earning his A.B. and M.D. from John Hopkins, John E. Eichenlaub served as Assistant Professor of Hygiene at the University of Illinois, and Associate Professor in the School of Public Health at the University of Minnesota.

Dr. Eichenlaub has written eight books, about 350 magazine articles, and more than 40 A.M.A. Journal articles. His books, which have sold over four million copies, have been translated into at least 12 languages. A MINNESOTA DOCTOR'S HOME REMEDIES FOR COMMON AND UNCOMMON AILMENTS *was on the New York Times' bestseller list.* THE MARRIAGE ART, NEW APPROACHES TO SEX IN MARRIAGE, *and* THE TROUBLED BED *have been widely sold.*

John E. Eichenlaub

Lord, let me raise children capable of achieving man-woman intimacy, and help them make the mutual commitments to reinforce that closeness. Let me leave them a world in which they can rear their own children, and substantially influence their children's development. Let me show them the broad horizons, the intense satisfactions, the keen fulfillments which marriage can breed, so that its struggles and its responsibilities will seem worthwhile.

❋ ❋ ❋

This is a humanitarian's prayer, not a parson's. My concern is not with marriage as a holy estate, but with its potential benefits for individuals, couples, families, and the world. Let's take a look at some of those benefits and at what we can do to enhance them, to see if they're worth the price of the struggle.

Hollywood plots Numbers 1, 5, and 7 assume that love is the bait, and that marriage is the snare. "After the honeymoon is over" and similar phrases constantly imply that shortly after marriage romance ceases, and only grim co-existence remains.

Yet marriage can be a lifelong intimate relationship, changing in nature from year to year, perhaps suffering occasional periods of strain, but still involving an enduring and deeply fulfilling emotional bond.

I have seen a few long-term loving relationships without benefit of marriage. The people involved cite benefits like these: *we keep trying to please each other all the time—never take each other for granted—prove and profess our love again and again.*

This sounds great until you stop to think about it. Then you begin to wonder. All that extra effort to please is based on anxiety—on fear of losing the loved one, and on uncertainty about whether the relationship could weather a storm. Do you really want to gain extra attentions from your mate at the price of uncertainty about whether he or she will still be with you next week? Is anxiety really a comfortable basis for a long-term relationship?

Like every other counselor, I have also seen couples who apparently got along fine until they were married, then developed deep-seated troubles. In the premarital phase, they generally "got along fine" (particularly on the sexual scene) because of lower expectations. The man expected sex only when the woman was entirely and spontaneously willing—regardless of his own pace. The woman expected full physical satisfaction only as occasional icing on the cake, instead of as her right. The couples who got along better *after* marriage than before have almost always done so on the basis of fuller communication, deeper intimacy, and a more relaxed, anxiety-free framework.

If there's any truth in the "honeymoon is over"

concept, it might be phrased: *"There's a time when every close relationship goes, at least, temporarily sour."* The Russians found this out when they made divorce as easy as sending a postcard—stable relationships seemed headed for limbo, along with occasionally-regretted covenants. So they reversed the practice with a vengeance. Ask any husband and wife who have built an enduring alliance, and they will tell you that at least a few times along the way only their feeling of commitment, *plus their desire not to fail in the socially imposed duty to make a marriage work,* kept them together.

"But why all this emphasis on *long term?"* you might ask. "So we might break up tomorrow; we're still in love today."

All right. Let's not talk about *duration,* let's talk about *intensity.* How deeply can a man and a woman love each other, and what contributes to that depth?

Love, to a great degree, is an act of trust. When you let someone become very important to you, you give him or her the power to wound you to the core. If a stranger insults you, you brush it off as nothing. The same insult from a friend hurts deeply; and the same insult from a true intimate may put you into a tailspin for weeks.

Most people cannot confer this power lightly—they might want to, and try to, and even think that they have, but the involuntary, foundation levels of the mind simply will not stand the risk. However, the rewards of deeper communication draw them gradually toward the tip of the limb; and if each hesitant overture gives further fulfillment without clear harm, they ultimately find truly intense intimacy.

"Long term" enters into this picture in two ways: Any reservations whatever, including those based on vague thoughts of prospective separation, make it more difficult to go all the way to full communication, and then to exposure and to hurt. Anyone who has gone that far, and then been spurned or rejected, finds it much more difficult to take the same steps again. A few very secure people can stand one or two rejections without pulling in their horns; but almost no one can wear his heart on his sleeve after several such episodes.

Moreover, love involves giving—the deep-down giving of self—which is difficult to manage outside the framework of assumed continuity. And love involves taking—the receiving what the other person offers, in spite of the awareness that this creates an obligation which is a blank check against your emotional account. Receiving assumes continued trustworthy relations through a period of time, too.

Unfortunately, a person who has not experienced the rewards of a truly close man-woman relationship has the same difficulty in perceiving them that a blind man has in seeing colors. This may be entirely a matter of individual makeup and values ("it just isn't my thing") or partly a variety of emotional sour grapes. Since such individuals can't tolerate a really close relationship, even through matrimony, which many of these people have tried without success, they turn a blind eye to the value of such a relationship. But the fact remains that perennial bachelors and bachelor girls don't say: "The kind of love you get in marriage isn't worth the confinement." They say: "There's nothing in marriage that I'm not getting already—absolutely nothing."

The silent majority still marry, stay married, and like it. Their overwhelming vote seems based on private joys and private fulfillments which, being too precious to expose, the non-initiates never see. But that does not mean those benefits don't exist. Married love is far from uniform and far from automatic, but *in toto* it yields more satisfactions than the popular myths assume.

One of the most moving passages in recent political oratory was Richard Nixon's tale of his poor immigrant father, who by hard work and sacrifice qualified his son for this nation's highest office. Whether or not we favor Nixon the Younger as President, all of us can appreciate Nixon Senior's feelings. We feel pride in our children's accomplishments and shame about their shortcomings, as well as joy in their pleasure, and sorrow at their pain.

This involvement with our children helps tremendously in getting the jobs of child-rearing and of education done. Children need love *first*, before they can possibly show love in return. They need love which counts it a privilege to give, and where the giver receives his rewards through involvement. They need the concerned care, the "prodigal child" tolerance, the college tuition checks, and all the rest.

"But why not adopt?" the modern generation asks.

Adoption works fairly well *in a framework of family values.* Most adoptive parents have been prepared throughout their lives for the paternal or maternal role, and need to occupy that role for deep-seated emotional reasons. They accept a substitute child because they have been brought up to feel that husband-wife-children constitute *the* biologically fulfilling unit. They develop attachment for the adopted child which over the years may become equivalent to that they would have had for a natural child, *but only because the family structure has provided the opportunity, the desire, and the groundwork.*

Assume a man-woman relationship which shuffles with every flicker of sexual interest, or assume social values which no longer identify with you the child you have reared, or assume "drafted" parents to replace the present "volunteers," and the adoptive family falls. As soon as a segment of society widely accepts illegitimacy and questions the sanctity of the family unit, its infants become dregs on the adoption market.

Moreover, the idea of the adoptive family is based on a very narrow, short-term conception of what a family is. If you think of the family only as "members of a household who are related by blood or marriage," the adoptive family becomes a fairly adequate replacement. But if you think of the family as a generations-long extension of self, or as a lasting institution of which you are merely the current standard-bearer, adoption becomes distinctly second best.

No one will die for his own pleasures or self-exercised privileges: only concern for future generations—basically for your own progeny—induces maximum sacrifice to build or to preserve the future. Moreover, the blood line family concept greatly enhances morality and achievement by making shame or pride broader and more crucial. And the blood line family provides opportunity on the one hand, security on the other, with no bureaucracy to administer either.

Natural families have one advantage over adoptive ones even under presently prevailing circumstances. The ideal relationship between parent and child involves *identification,* which means that your involvement affects your self-esteem. You feel proud of a loved one's achievements and ashamed of his failures or crimes. That pride or that shame, as the case might be, is a crucial part of your love. No matter how you might try to treat an adoptive child like a natural one, there simply isn't as great an involvement in this respect as with an extension of your own genetic presence on this earth.

In an emotionally unrewarding marriage, responsibilities loom large. The breadwinner can think of a thousand ways to spend his money which would yield him greater satisfaction than maintaining a household which he does not particularly enjoy. The housekeeper counts the returns from her hours of drudgery and compares them unfavorably with the going industrial wage. Although these roles are not necessarily strictly male and female anymore, it adds up to a bad bargain, no matter how you cut the deal.

But the responsibilities of marriage are the price you pay for deeper, more stable love and privileged parenthood. If these rewards yield enough fulfillment, the chores of marriage seem a reasonable bargain.

Moreover, those chores seem much less onerous in a soundly functioning marriage. The happiness your wife gets from a new dress is reflected in your own satisfaction. That happiness might amount to more than you could get by spending the money on yourself. Ideal marital give and take is not reciprocal but simultaneous —instead of merely giving to get, you also get by the act of giving.

* * *

To judge an institution like marriage, you have to consider what it might contribute in the future. While I admit to charges of incurable optimism, I would judge the prospects to be rather good for two reasons.

First: The newer, more open attitudes about discussion and disclosure of sexual matters must spread to happily married people within the next few years, if only through the arrival of liberally reared young people of marriageable age. My personal prognostication is that this event will produce a vast surge in the esteem for matrimony.

For many years, Victorian prudery has persisted in a most irrational form. Conversation has flowed freely regarding perverted sex, premarital sex, extramarital sex and so forth; but one subject has remained utterly and totally taboo: good, wholesome physical intimacy between a husband and a wife. This taboo is especially strong after their children have reached the age of even vague sophistication.

Why does such reticence seem irrational? Because we want to serve as models for our youngsters—to give them a working, emulatable example of a man-woman relationship. Concealing all evidence of intimacy grossly distorts their view.

And because we want our children to accept us as qualified advisers in man-woman relationships. Giving the impression that we are no longer active sexual beings makes us seem out of touch.

And because we want our children to think of sex as a long-run phenomenon, not the exclusive property of the under 30's. If we conceal our own continuing joys and satisfactions, we weight the scales in favor of "gather ye rosebuds while ye may," as opposed to building toward a lifetime of building mutuality and fulfillment.

And because the very cornerstone of neurosis is the feeling that all intimate relations help compete directly with each other. An awareness of sexual intimacy between one's parents helps a child distinguish the qualitative difference between spousal and parent-child relationships, and helps the child recognize the essentially noncompetitive nature of these relationships.

I would venture to predict that marriage will be much stronger, and that the generation gap will be much less when parents let their children know about their continuing physical intimacy. Improved couple communications, greater general respect for married people as sexual beings, and better attitudes of succeeding generations toward marriage should all follow when people recognize happily married couples as sex partners. Parents, too, are sexual beings. Young people must learn to understand that campus lovers are merely fumbling neophytes by comparison with at least some of their elders.

My second reason for thinking that marriage will move up instead of down is the dawning awareness in our society of the true conflict between the freedom of an individual and the freedom of a family. This idea seems to rumble around in the basement of political pronouncements instead of being cried from the towers, but I believe it is on the rise.

If I as a father have a right to boost my children into a better position than they would have reached through their own gumption and ability, then whomever they displace is being deprived of his rights as an individual. If, on the other hand, I have difficulty providing opportunity for my family because of taxes being used to rear somebody else's bastards, then the individual rights of certain children are being given a higher priority than my family unit's. Society cannot let the bastards starve, but considerable disquietude seems to be arising about the notion that they deserve everything a loving father could have given them. I firmly believe that the pendulum will swing back to a degree of family-based opportunity, and that a stronger association of family with position and achievement will help to sustain both the natural family and the rites of marriage by which parent-child relations are publicly acknowledged.

My vote on marriage is resoundingly *for;* and my plea is not for changes in the institution, but for greater support of marriage in the educational, the social, and the legal spheres. Unfortunately, we have never faced up to the dilemmas in each of these areas which arise when freedom for families and freedom for individuals conflict.

Recent emphasis on individual freedom has made marriage in some respects a bad deal. As long as you are not part of a family, you get all kinds of services from governmental and other agencies which members of a family have to provide for themselves. As long as you don't actually marry, feminine equality can be interpreted as *"shift for yourself if we separate."* The concept of "equal opportunity" takes the neglectful father off the hook.

But the gains we can make through marriage and certified family connection seem to me so great and so frequently attainable that they fully justify the price.

Let's stop hiding the light of married love under a bushel basket, letting our desire to give individuals a break undermine the family-centered basis for our culture, and chasing will-of-the-wisps like the adoptive family or the three-year renewable marriage contract on the assumption that all the good in our society will stay the same, even if we drastically change the rules.

Ira L. Reiss is Professor of Sociology and Director of the Family Study Center at the University of Minnesota. His primary interests are in the area of the sociology of the family and the study of deviant behavior. In 1970, he was elected President of the Mid-west Sociological Society.

He has done extensive research using both national and local samples, and is at present undertaking research in the area of marital dissolution.

Professor Reiss has published several books including: PREMARITAL SEXUAL STANDARDS IN AMERICA, THE SOCIAL CONTEXT OF PREMARITAL SEXUAL PERMISSIVENESS, and THE FAMILY SYSTEM IN AMERICA. He has served as associate editor on the AMERICAN SOCIOLOGICAL REVIEW, SOCIAL PROBLEMS, and JOURNAL OF MARRIAGE AND THE FAMILY.

Ira L. Reiss

THE MONTHLY REPORTS from the Federal Government indicate that the divorce rate is continuing to rise at a speed that hasn't been equaled since World War I. Except for 1946, divorce rates have not risen more than a total of 30% between 1920 and 1965. But since 1965, the divorce rate has climbed by over 40%! Is this a a sign that American marriage is on the way out?

Increasingly, one reads reports of young people's living together without having been legally married. Social scientists report studies of mate exchanges occurring in most of our major urban centers, with the help of commercial clubs and newspaper advertisements. Communal forms of living and communal forms of childrearing are appearing all over the country. Women's liberation groups and zero population growth organizations are promoting the joys of single life as compared with married life.

Since divorce is one of the most frequently cited evidences of marital demise, let us examine it first. All societies have some way in which people can relieve the stress of an unhappy marriage. One way out is by having multiple mates; another, by permitting concubinage. Unhappy women have been told to focus their lives on their children. And, of course, there's been divorce. Divorce enables one to break off completely the unhappy relationship, and so possibly find someone else with whom a relatively happy relationship can be established.

California and Iowa have recently allowed for divorce in cases where a marriage is "irretrievable." In these states, the process of having to prove the guilt of one party is not involved. Many other states, too, have eased the requirements for divorce since in today's society, divorce bears but little social stigma. Thus, the rise in the divorce rate may be simply an indicator of how many people are leaving unhappy marriages. Widening the exit doors can dramatically affect this statistic.

Also today, with the stress on self-expression and self-realization, divorce is usually regarded as a perfectly legitimate way to end undue stress. The really interesting statistic would be one that informed us what proportion of all marriages were happy and were meeting the major needs of the persons involved. This proportion could be very low, and divorce could still be very low, if society had other means for resolving marital dissatisfaction.

For example, in Italy the recent debate over allowing divorce led to the revelation of some rather high rates of bigamy. Since divorce was illegal, an unhappy mate would leave and marry someone else. Others would simply live with the new partner in a consensual union and not be legally married.

If one wants to appraise the state of a marriage, the measure of the actual commitment and the needs being fulfilled in that relationship are much more to

the point than whether either of the parties has
sought divorce. In a tight divorce situation, many unhappy people do not seek divorce. It is likely that the
proportion of those today who are happily married is at
an all-time high, since those who are dissatisfied with
their marriage can so easily leave it.

Since 1930, European countries have increasingly
adopted our type of free, open courtship, and our
system of marriage for love. Since that time European
divorce rates have risen at a much higher rate than
our own. The divorce rates in Europe have not reached
ours as yet, but the gap is closing. When one marries
because he believes that a close emotional relation
will continue for many years, then, when the error of
that choice is revealed, there is little in the way of
parental control, religious control, or a sense of duty
that can counteract the drive to seek an end to that
union.

In most cases, the divorced person continues the
search for a suitable mate; and in fact, divorced people
marry at a faster rate than do single people of the
same age.

Most second marriages last. Persons who have
divorced more than once are a small minority. Only 6%
of the marriages in any year involve persons who
have been twice divorced. However, second marriages
do seem to have a higher rate of divorce than do first
marriages.

Almost 80% of American 50-year-old white males
are living with their first wives, and over half of the

black males of the same age are also living with their first wives.[1]

With easy mobility out of marriage, and with more rapid remarriage—half of those who remarry do so in two or three years after their divorce—it seems that divorce underscores the search for marital happiness and is not necessarily a sign that marriage as an institution is disintegrating. Just as broken engagements may be a necessary part of the courtship search process, broken marriages may also be an essential part of the search for marital happiness. While a minority may use the divorce process excessively, most people use it sparingly. Overall then, divorce is not a good index of whether or not marriage is dying; rather divorce may well be a sign of the seriousness with which the members of our society are seeking a good marriage.

*   *   *

There are those who view marriage as the legitimation of sexual relationships. In our society, most individuals engage in premarital intercourse; and most men also engage in extramarital intercourse. In many other societies, this is even more so the case. Though it is true that sex is prescribed as a part of marriage, sex is easily available in some fashion outside of marriage. So it seems clear that legitimation of sex is not the key function of marriage.

[1] Reiss, Ira L.: THE FAMILY SYSTEM IN AMERICA, Holt, Rinehart and Winston, Inc., 1971.

As Malinowski observed many decades ago, marriage has the key function of legitimizing parenthood.[2] Marriage, in effect, is the group's way of sanctioning two or more people as future parents. The same child, born to the same couple but without the sanction of marriage, is an illegitimate child.

If we change marriage to a ceremony with a rock band, or if we hold that the sharing of a room signifies marriage, then we are not eliminating marriage, but rather just changing the form of its consummation. To be called a marriage, there must be more than a sexual relationship; there must be the acceptance of the potential parental role.

A good case in point is the current discussion about "living together" on our college campuses. There always have been college couples who shared apartments; but today, the proportion of students involved appears to have increased considerably.

Two questions must be raised here: First: Is this a form of marriage? Secondly: If not, is this a sign that marriage is dying? The evidence would indicate negative answers.

One of the few studies of couples, living together, was done by Michael Johnson at an Iowa college campus a few years ago.[3] Johnson matched 19 unmarried

[2] Malinowski, Bronislaw: THE SEXUAL LIFE OF SAVAGES IN NORTH-WESTERN MELANESIA. Harvest Books, 1929.

[3] Johnson, Michael P.: "Courtship and Commitment: A study of Cohabitation on a University Campus." Master's Thesis, unpublished, University of Iowa, 1969.

couples, living together, with 19 married couples. One of the most interesting findings was that most of the unmarried couples, intended someday to get legally married, although not necessarily to the person they were living with. Most of these couples did not view their living together as a substitute for marriage, but rather as a part of a courtship. A common view was that it was hypocritical to take a girl back to her abode after copulating, just so others wouldn't have direct evidence that a sexual affair was occurring. These people generally felt it was simpler and more honest to live with someone with whom one was having an affair. These unmarried couples did not want children. Here again, the evidence was that living together was not a substitute for marriage.

Now, let us assume that the feelings of those Iowa couples were not typical of the norm and that most such couples do not plan to get legally married at any time; but do, in fact, want to have children—then what? Then, could you say that marriage for these couples was a dead institution?

A simple arrangement such as living together is often the way in which a marriage is announced. This is a common way in the Israeli kibbutzim.[4] The simplicity of the arrangement, then has no bearing on whether or not it is marriage; what matters is whether there is evidence that the two persons involved are

---

[4] Spiro, Melford E.: KIBBUTZ: VENTURE IN UTOPIA, Harvard University Press, 1956.

sanctioned as future parents. The findings from Johnson indicate that persons who live together do, indeed,
have standards, and do view affection as quite important. I feel certain that incest taboos, age limitations, mental retardation, and other factors also enter
into the consideration as to who is an acceptable future parent. Thus, if we did have couples living
together who did not want to get legally married but
who eventually wanted to have children, then such
persons cannot be said to be opposed to marriage.
Theirs would be a different type of marriage than the
form we have now, but it would still function as the
legitimation of parenthood.

I doubt whether such an arrangement will become
too popular in America, simply because the legal
aspects of life are too complicated for such an arrangement. Even in the Israeli kibbutzim, legal marriages
are often performed for legal reasons at the time of the
birth of the first child. My guess is that living together
before a couple wants children will become increasingly popular, but that legal marriage when the woman
becomes pregnant will remain by far the dominant
mode.

*   *   *

Back in the 1940's, Kinsey found that by age 40
about 50% of the men and 26% of the women had
participated in extramarital intercourse.[5] The rates to-

[5] Kinsey, Alfred C., et. al.: SEXUAL BEHAVIOR IN THE HUMAN FEMALE,
W. B. Saunders and Co., 1953.

day are probably somewhat higher. What does this imply about the quality of American marriage and its likely future?

The double standard seems present in most areas of male-female interaction. A male is much more likely to cite adultery by his mate as reason for divorce than is a female. However, some trends toward equalitarianism are noticeable.

Both men and women seem able to tolerate their own adultery, but find it much more difficult to tolerate the adultery of their partners. It seems that adultery with a person for whom one does *not* have deep affection is the kind of adultery most tolerated by the one's spouse.[6] This is likely so because such adultery poses less of a threat to a marriage.

Swinging is generally understood as sexual activity involving two or more married couples, where access to each other's mates is mutually agreed upon. Such mate exchange is not unknown outside the Western world. Some of the Eskimo tribes used to while away the long winter months by playing a game called "putting out the lamps," which involved several couples in one shelter putting out the oil lamps and scrambling for a sex partner for the night.[7] The normative expectation today in American swinging is that there be very

[6] Christensen, Harold T.: "A Cross-Cultural Comparison of Attitudes Toward Marital Infidelity," *International Journal of Comparative Sociology* 1962, pp. 124-137.

[7] Reiss, Ira L.: PREMARITAL SEXUAL STANDARDS IN AMERICA, The Free Press, 1960.

little emotional involvement between the sex partners, and that they do not see each other, apart from the party occasions. In short, it is an affectionless scene, and thus, very much in line with the greater acceptability of extramarital coitus which lacks affection. Also, swinging integrates with the increased equalitarianism, since it affords the female equal sexual rights with the male. Often, wives report that they were not fully willing when they began; but after some experience, it may be the husband—and not the wife—who becomes disillusioned and wants to stop swinging.[8]

Swinging does not integrate well with one feature of our value system: the notion that romantic love should be exclusive and possessive. Romantic love traditionally has had a view that the loved one belonged to you and you alone, and that the sharing of intimate experiences violated the relationship. This is not to say that some kinds of love and swinging cannot mix.

If sex could be treated as casually as one might treat playing golf or watching football, a husband might be willing to share his wife's enjoyment of sex with others, and vice versa. But such a couple would have to reject the possessive view of love.

It does seem to me, however, that when one derives emotional and physical rewards from sexual intercourse with someone, an affectionate relationship

[8] Bartell, Gilbert: "Group Sex Among the Mid-American," *The Journal of Sex Research* May, 1970, 113-130.

frequently develops. This new meaningful relationship means the loss of full sexual priority previously held by one's mate. Further, sexual attraction to another person and the pursuit of pleasure may also reduce the focus of a husband and wife upon each other. Thus, I do not believe that swinging can be easily combined with a "totalistic," romantic love relationship. It may more easily be combined with less possessive relationships.

However, if sex jealously can be removed from the realm of marriage, then swinging may increase overall sexual and emotional satisfactions for both husband and wife. This is possible in a less romantic and more limited type of love relationship.

How likely are certain consequences to occur? In what type of encounter? In what type of marriage? Extramarital coitus is clearly something different for someone married to a handicapped mate, or bogged down in an unhappy marriage, or separated for a long time from his mate than it is for someone who is happily married and living with his mate. Extramarital coitus is different when both partners *know* what is going on and are agreeable to the arrangement than it is when one partner conceals the fact.

The greater the freedom of expression, the higher the levels of temptation, and the greater the female's interest in sex, the more likely that we'll have higher adultery rates. But—and this is the key question—does this overall cultural change predispose toward unhappier marriages? I don't think so. I think this situation leads to greater openness and honesty and to a greater likelihood of discussion about sexual choices. One result is likely to be more experimenting, but I would guess that the number of significant and rewarding marriage relationships will increase.

Some people have viewed the growth of communal living groups and communal child-rearing arrangements as evidence of the demise of marriage. But, as stated above, such arrangements may be part of a system to legitimize certain persons as potential parents. In the Israeli kibbutzim, children are reared communally and do not reside with their parents. But the parents live together, and act out socially accepted husband and wife roles. Thus, marriage does exist. Furthermore, the parental tie to the children is very intense. In many ways, one could describe this society as child-centered, despite the communal upbringing outside of the home. Also, the tie of affection between husband and wife is a highly valued part of their life style. Such communal arrangements are not inimical to marriage.

Bennett Berger's reports on his ongoing study of California communes is very informative.[9] He has limited himself to rural communes that have been in existence for at least six months, and thus his findings may not apply to other communes. He found that although there was verbal tolerance for sexual experimentation, very little went on, and that the married

[9] Berger, Bennett, et. al.: "Child Rearing Practices of the Communal Family," pp. 509-523 in: Arlene S. Skolnick and Jerome H. Skolnick (eds.) FAMILY IN TRANSITION. Little Brown and Co., 1971.

couples were not so tolerant. He also found that the chores, such as cooking, cleaning, and child-care, were typically performed by females, not by males.

Thus, the commune picture that emerges is not one of radical change in marital relations. The radical change seems to be in the attempt to achieve close relations in *one* household, *among a relatively large number of people*. This is a departure from the suburban nuclear family ranch house, but in many other ways, it is not a departure from conventional marriage. Perhaps, in time, with a second generation on the commune scene, more radical changes will appear. But even so, it looks as though some form of marriage is well ensconced in the commune setting.

Larry and Joan Constantine have been investigating couples who live in arrangements of polygamous marriage.[10] They have found a few dozen couples who live in a variety of such arrangements. But even in such unions, if they became a way of socially recognizing persons as potential parents, we would still have a marriage system.

Equally important is their finding that such unions were extremely unstable. Jealousy, conflict, loss of interest, and other factors have operated to dissolve such marriages rather quickly.

The complexity of multiple matings, where there are multiple mates of both sexes, can be cross-culturally

[10] Constantine, Joan and Larry: Where is Marriage Going? *The Futurist* April, 1970, pp. 44-46.

supported. Polygamy is a very common marriage form around the world. It is almost always in the specific mode of one husband and several wives; only in rare cases is there one wife with several husbands. The logical possibility of several wives and several husbands is found only as an optional practice, and then in only extremely rare instances. It would seem that the complexity of multiple mates of both sexes is simply too much to handle for people in almost all social systems.

Also, one must decide what he wants out of a relationship. If one desires a close intimate relationship, then there are limits as to how many people in various roles this can be achieved with. If one is willing to participate in a mechanical, more bureaucratized type of relationship with various people, then greater numbers can be added.

It is difficult for even two people to be able to live together intimately for many years. I would think that it is even more difficult when you increase the number of individuals involved. So I do not think our marriage form will change to any considerable extent in a polygamous direction. Most likely, only a few groups will live in polygamous arrangements. But even if polygamy became widespread, it should be clear that polygamy is a form of marriage, and this would not augur the end of marriage as an institution.

*   *   *

People today are able to act and to talk more as

they really feel. Those most likely to be disturbed by extramarital coitus are those least likely to try varied sexual adventures. I view this rise in the openness with which adultery is discussed by married couples as a change that may well aid in the growth of more rational attitudes toward extramarital coitus; it is quite analogous to the development of discussion of legitimate choices in premarital coitus. Both developments are a sign of an increase in the moral choices being made today, and a decrease in the emotional compulsive behavior in the past regarding sex. Greater female permissiveness premaritally increases the supply of extramarital sex partners. In this sense, too, the changes in premarital sex relate to changes in extramarital sex. I do not see the changes in adultery patterns as a sign of the end of marriage, but rather as a growth of rational discussion in an important moral area.

*   *   *

We are in a period of exploration. More ways for people to meet, marry, live, and raise children have been explored in the 1960's than in any other decade of our history. I suspect that this opening of doors has disturbed some people who view our marriage system in a rather narrow way, and that this uneasiness has led to the feeling that marriage is declining in importance, and in time may even cease to exist. I happen to believe that rational exploration of all possibilities is the most promising way of arriving at a style of life that will yield the greatest satisfaction.

Perhaps it is those who fear that their particular way will not hold up in such a rational light who oppose the examination of alternatives.

I believe that the 1970's will witness a period in which people will come to know the nature of the various alternatives. Then the choosing will become more routinized.

Enlarging the scope of choice will have the long-run consequence of greater acceptability of variety. Never again can we picture only the two-parent family as the healthy family, or regard divorce as disgraceful, or condemn premarital coitus as disastrous.

We will witness more people who will live together but never marry. We will find more couples who marry but who never have children. We will find more women with small children who work full time. We will encounter fewer unwanted children. And so forth.

The bulk of the people will likely choose to marry, to have children, and to live in nuclear family households. But those who choose to marry and not have children, and those who live in communal households will also find social acceptance.

I do not see full equality of the sexes within the next few decades, although dramatic changes in that direction will occur. The men who most favor equality for women are career men who would not often take the time to share fully in the child-rearing and household tasks. The lower class men and women who have less career orientation are less equalitarian. Nevertheless, strong inroads will be made toward more equality of the sexes. Yet in the year 2,000, I believe there will still be many more women than men in the home taking care of small children. However, we will also have many more women in all walks of life than ever before; and our social productivity will show the worth of this change.[11]

Perhaps, in conclusion, I should note some of the risks involved in the new life styles. The major risk in opening up choice is error in choice. When choices open up, one must carefully consider priorities. The older restricted system exacted a price: it placed a person in a mold which did not enable him to choose a life style that would allow maximum self-growth and social contribution. The current, more open system runs the risk of one's acting impulsively. Such precipitate action might destroy aspects of life of higher priority. For example, one may impulsively get involved in a sexual encounter, and thereby cause a break in a meaningful relationship; or one may hastily get involved in divorce proceedings, and thereby avoid facing up to faults in oneself. Thus, the price of a more open system is the greater need for a rational examination of the alternatives.

The old system had many people trapped in a rut; the new one may have many people constantly running from one style of life to another, unable to choose wisely.

[11] Thompson, Mary Lou (ed.): VOICES OF THE NEW FEMINISM. Beacon Press, 1970.

The advantage of the new system is that it affords the greater opportunity for finding oneself. Marriage in the new society can be a most exciting relationship, but it will remain a relationship that needs constant reflective attention. This generation of young people is being given a range of choices far beyond that given to any other generation, but such a choice demands that the young exercise a maturity beyond that of previous generations.[12]

New demands now also fall on older married couples, as they come to be influenced by the changing social setting. It is an exciting time both for the participants and for sociologists like myself who have the opportunity to study this new dynamic social context of marriage.

[12] Reiss, Ira L.: THE SOCIAL CONTEXT OF PREMARITAL SEXUAL PERMISSIVENESS, Holt, Rinehart and Winston, Inc., 1967.

A sociologist who specializes in adolescents, young adults, and sex education, Carlfred B. Broderick teaches courses in family relations and sexual behavior at The Pennsylvania State University. He also serves as an adviser to graduate students in the fields of child development and family relationships.

Dr. Broderick is the editor of "Journal of Marriage and the Family," a quarterly publication of the National Council on Family Relations, and is the co-editor of a new reference book for sex educators entitled THE INDIVIDUAL, SEX AND SOCIETY. His book SEXUAL DEVELOPMENT IN CHILDHOOD AND YOUTH has been published in English, German, Dutch, and Italian. He has authored numerous articles for professional and popular publications.

Carlfred B. Broderick

EVEN THOSE WHO FIND the least to admire in the institution of marriage must admit that, like cockroaches and crabgrass, it is extraordinarily durable and ubiquitous. Indeed, if there is any society, past or present, primitive or civilized, in which marriage was not the preferred living arrangement for adults, it has escaped the attention of scholars.

Despite the general popularity of marriage, or perhaps because of it, philosophers over the ages have sought to design a nobler arrangement. Plato found the common pattern of a man's and a woman's living together and raising children to be lacking in perfection, and he suggested a Republic based on a higher principle. St. Paul acknowledged that it was better to marry than to burn, but urged all with any spiritual stamina to accept a more godly celibacy. Engles found that marriage imprisoned and exploited women, reducing them to the status of serfs; and he preached a new classless society where each worker would stand in direct relation to the economy and the state, unencumbered by domestic tyranny.

Plato fathered a civilization; St. Paul and his writings converted the Western World; Engles helped launch the great working class revolutions of our century, not to mention Women's Lib. None of them made much of a dent in the universality of marriage.

Thus, there would seem to be little cause for the friends of marriage to panic in the face of the currently fashionable attacks upon this venerable institution. It has demonstrated its evolutionary toughness, and for millennia, it has established its competitive advantage in the arena of man's life decisions. It is difficult to imagine its yielding now to Rimmer's *Proposition 31*.[1]

Nevertheless, it may be profitable to examine the charges made against marriage by its current detractors, and to evaluate the evidence that new life arrangements are about to replace it.

One of the chief current complaints against marriage is that it very often fails to provide the full measure of romantic bliss it advertises. Perhaps no other society has ever promised so much return on such a small investment. Fall in love and get married, we say, and rich treasures of personal fulfillment and contentment will follow.

Since happiness and success are at a premium in every arena of life, it is fair to ask how this social fiction developed as a mechanism for moving young people into marriage. I am myself persuaded by the view that every society has an investment in articulating its young into the larger social system. Generally, this has meant initiation into the world of work for the male, and into the world of family responsibilities for both male and female.

In traditional society, a family took an active role

[1] R. H. Rimmer: PROPOSITION 31, NAL, 1969

in moving its children into adult roles. Gradually, due to the increased emphasis on individual freedom, the power of the parents over their young adult children lessened, and those mechanisms which relied upon internalized motivations increased in importance.

As a strategy to make marriage attractive, society conspired to picture marriage as the only arrangement which could assure love, sex, companionship, stability, peace, and happiness. In order for this to be a credible expectation, of course, it was also necessary to sponsor a type of irrational blindness to the plentiful evidence that marriage—while an exceptionally sensible arrangement—could scarcely guarantee paradise in an all too mortal relationship.

It is curious that as our sophisticated younger generation has pierced the hypocrisy of the romantic myth of marriage, rather than taking a more pragmatic view of human relationships in general, they have merely transferred their romanticism to other institutions: for example, the commune.

The great secret about marriage is that, while it has enormous potential for the development of intense and rewarding relationships, its stability as an institution does not at all depend upon that potential. Marriage is, above all, a relatively stable and sensible contractual living arrangement for pairs of adults. They agree to share bed and board, to exchange services without recompense, to support each other emotionally and economically, and to take joint responsibility for any children they may have. They also agree to forsake and forego such other relationships which would undermine the marriage.

It is not too surprising that many find the romantic freight which such arrangements are required to bear too great a burden. Some pairs become disillusioned and break up, while many more stay married, though disenchanted. Cuber and Harroff have categorized the majority of middle-aged marriages as having passed from vital romantic relationships into passive congenial or devitalized or even conflict-habituated status. Nevertheless, lacking a more attractive alternative life-style, people in these categories tend to stay married.

One word about the divorce rate which continues to rise. Many have suggested that this increase shows a growing disenchantment with marriage as a style of life. This is manifestly baseless since no one gets married more quickly than a divorcee. That is, if one takes divorcees, widows, and never-marrieds of the same age, the divorcees are the first to get married; the widows, next; and the never-marrieds, last. Thus, although the number of divorces per year is currently almost one-third as great as the number of marriages per year, those who are in divorced status in any given year is well under 5%.

It is clear that it is not marriage as a way of life that is repudiated by the divorcee, but that disappointing spouse. And so, with the hope that perhaps the romantic ideal may be realized the next time around, the divorcee rejoins the vast majority who have found the marital state—on balance—better than the alternatives. Surely, no greater testimonial to marriage could be found.

Another charge leveled at marriage is that it inhibits personal freedom and self-actualization for both men and women—but especially for women. The charge is true to the extent that every commitment and every institution, by definition, limits alternatives.

The more relevant question is whether marriage is worth the price. Are the rewards of marriage sufficient to justify the loss of autonomy which marital and familial ties impose? Most people seem to think so.

Yet it is true that our society is increasingly shifting toward a thoroughly existential value system instead of a system anchored in institutions. Fewer people are concerned with preserving the religious or political or domestic arrangements of the past. Rather, they would maximize the intensity of their experiences, and their freedom of personal choice. Especially among the youth, "doing your thing" and permitting others the same privilege is considered very nearly the ultimate value.

It is increasingly common for those of this persuasion to take it for granted that a revolution against the Establishment is both desirable and inevitable. In that millennial day, all of the present institutions will be done away with, and people will be free, at last, to do what they want to do, unencumbered with the strictures which have inhibited man's development in the past.

For this group, traditional marital and family arrangements are a double enemy. These institutions not only enslave men and women through law, custom, and economic oppression, but they pass these same values and institutions onto their children. For this reason, every revolutionary has found himself in opposition to the family.

Plato realized that if he were ever to achieve his Utopia, he would have to take children away from their families and raise them communally. Jesus of Nazareth preached that if anyone were not willing to hate his father and mother and brother and sister for the sake of this new gospel, he was not worthy to be a disciple. Engles and Marx saw the need to put the children in state nurseries and schools, if they were going to become good Communists. And, currently, we put children into *Headstart* and *Upward Bound* programs to get them away from their parents' influence, and so break the cycle of poverty.

However, each of these efforts to supplant the family has failed because the cost of eliminating the family as a social mechanism has proved to be too great. The case of the Israeli kibbutz is especially instructive, particularly because it was most carefully worked out. In order to establish a new way of life in which men and women could be equal, Eastern European Jews emigrated to Israel and set up farming cooperatives. Using great intelligence and commitment, they arranged for rotating assignments to tasks, and for community care of their children. For a generation, the kibbutz was hailed as a successful model for all social innovations. Yet, in the second generation, the tasks of this community have developed into traditional sex typing; and today, young parents are asserting their parental prerogatives vis-a-vis the community.

Why? What competitive advantage does the traditional arrangement of husband and wife, parents and children, have that can account for its re-emergence in the kibbutz, and in Soviet Russia, and in primitive Christianity?

One answer is that freedom is not an ultimate value, and that human relatedness is. This point is recognized by the revolutionaries, but they feel that many forms of human connectedness could meet this fundamental human need better than marriage and the family. The new suggested arrangements would be intense and multifaceted, but they would provide for easy exit and entrance, thus avoiding the oppressive nature of long-term, exclusive commitments.

But the point is that it is precisely the exclusivity and the durability of marriage that give it its competitive advantage. Every study of personality development has showed that being raised in a stable and unthreatened emotional environment is most conducive to developing ego strength and social competence in children.

It is reasonable to believe that this is also true for adults. Erickson suggests that autonomy follows basic trust in the development of personality. That is, the child or the adult who is secure in his home relationship sallies forth into the world with more confidence and resource than the child or the adult who has to keep one

foot and one eye at home all the time because his
security there may blow up at any time.

It is also not at all clear whether the traditional
life-cycle events of marriage, parenthood, and launch-
ing a family can be improved upon as vehicles of self-
actualization. Each requires personal growth; each
demands the development of altruism; each challenges
the status quo, pushing the individual onto new levels
of maturity. Not all find equal profit in this classic
sequence, but no other sequence has been shown to be
more effective in inducing growth in individuals.

Perhaps the most persuasive argument against the
survival of traditional marriage is that galloping technology has, for the first time in history, made it possible
to divorce sexual relationships from reproduction. Although it is admitted that this has not been fully
achieved as yet, we are assured that the ideal contraceptive is just around the corner; that before too long,
artificial insemination and extra-uterine pregnancies a la
Brave New World will have replaced the traditional
modes of conception and childbearing.

Assuming for the moment that all of these technological marvels are, in fact, achieved in the near
future, what might the consequences for our familiar
arrangement be? The answer immediately given, these
days, is that sex—once freed from reproductive encum-
brance—will become the chief sacrament of interpersonal togetherness.

As many have rushed forward to observe, there is
no special reason why such non-reproductive together-

ness need be restricted to enduring heterosexual pairs. Indeed, celebrants need be related neither enduringly, heterosexually, nor in pairs. The only restriction which most would endorse is that the participants be consenting adults. Inevitably, there is already a group in Southern California which proposes to extend these sacraments of togetherness to children. Their rationale is that if sex is divorced from social consequences, there would seem to be no reason to restrict sex to adults.

Perhaps this analysis is correct, and man is a creature of his technology. Myself, I cannot help noting that what is technologically possible does not necessarily become universally adopted. Sex has always served many functions for man, including personal pleasure and relational support. Undoubtedly, sex will continue to do so, perhaps on an expanded basis. But what the anti-family social prophets expect us to believe is that sex will cease to function as a focal point of continuing, exclusive, heterosexual unions, and that sex will be replaced as the chief mechanism of reproduction.

It seems to me that the weight of human nature is against these prophets. I am willing to believe that the day may come when babies can be conceived and brought forth without any contact between father and mother, or between mother and fetus. I am not willing to believe that any society will *choose* to produce its young in that way.

There have always been alternatives to marriage, although it is true that our own cultural tradition provided poorly for the unmarried. The traditional alternatives continue today, except that, today, some of the romanticism and legitimacy that used to be attached to marriage is attached to these alternatives too. Always there has been consensual union. In many states, such an arrangement was provided with common law protection. Always there has been the bachelor or the spinster who lives alone, but may involve himself or herself in a heterosexual or a homosexual affair. Always there has been the extended kin group, or the pseudo-kin group, whether it be called a *commune* or a *group* or a *gang*. But always the vast majority of us have been organized into marital units.

I cannot help wondering whether we have not been deceived by the short-range perspective of the young on these matters. College and high school students are, by societal design, between two family stages in their life cycle. They are encouraged to assert their independence from their parental family, and there is little to encourage them to take upon themselves the responsibilities of marriage and a family before they get established in a trade or a profession. If they accept money from their parents to help to establish a new family, they violate the norm of independence from their parents. If they quit school to work, they jeopardize their future. It is small wonder that this lonely, unarticulated age group has become fascinated by the exploration of innovative living styles for themselves. Nor is it surprising, in view of the politicizing of the young, that they rationalize their solutions with revolutionary rhetoric and a great deal of provocative noisemaking.

What is disappointing is that the professors and mentors of the young have become captivated by the rhetoric all around them, and have accorded such talk the weight of social philosophy. Soon, academicians will be able to footnote not only their students, but each other; and before we are truly aware of what's going on, the jury-rigged solutions of an age group suspended between institutional commitments, will have been declared the wave of the future for all of us.

I would rather wait and see what happens to these revolutionary life forms in the lives of these same students. I think I see the life forms continuing, but the students themselves graduating—or if you prefer, dropping out—into marriage and family responsibilities.

Marriage, like cockroaches and crabgrass, has been around a long time; and I'm betting on its being around a still longer time.

Index

Index

pride, 229
Prince of Wales, 119
Princeton, 175
privacy, 58, 109, 157
procreation, 192
"prodigal child," 227
productiveness, 140
promiscuity, 94
 orgiastic, 103
property, 104
 sharing, 105
PROPOSITION 31, 254
prostitution, 97-98, 207
psyche, 49, 102, 186
psychiatrists, 148
psychic survival, 139
psychologists, 74, 148
puberty, 199
public morals, 118
Puritanism, new, 172, 173
"putting out the lamps," 242

quadrads, 219, 220
Quaker, 173

radical chicks, 51
"radiclibs," 62

READER'S DIGEST, 48
reciprocity, 216, 217
recreation, 144, 190
reform, 63
refuge, 47
Reiss, Ira L., 234-251
relationships, 104, 157, 160,
 162, 165, 200, 214, 219, 260
 awareness of time in, 158
 biological, 164
 casual, 174
 dyadic, 218
 exclusive, 63
 family-like, 217
 interpersonal, 71, 197
 involuntary, 145
 life-long, 153, 158, 163, 223
 love, 197, 244
 network of, 71
 psycho-sexual, 154, 155, 158
 quadrad, 219, 220
 sex, 203, 238
 social, 213, 215
 "totalistic," 244
 triad, 107, 219, 220
religion, 31, 64, 96, 191
religious
 ideals, 67
 nurture, 190
remarriage, 65, 98, 109, 122,
 123, 218, 238
 falling divorce rate in, 98
Rembrandt, 163
repression, 95
reproduction, 193, 197, 260

asexual, 195
resignation, 41
responsibility, 163
revolution
  erotic, 102
  working class, 253
"right of privacy," 43
rights
  of the sexes, 119, 149
  property, 86
  reciprocal, 79
  sexual, 90
  women's struggle for equal,
    117
rigidity, 95
Rimmer, Robert H., 73, 254
ritual, 47, 203
rivalries, 106
rock, 39
role playing, 54, 55
roles, 229-230
  voluntary and spontaneous,
    105
romance, 143, 197, 200
  method, 146
romanticism, 196, 261-262
romanticize, 51, 52, 53, 55
Roy, Rustum, 60-76
Royal Commission of 1912, 118
Royal Commission on Divorce,
  113
  findings of, 113-115
Russell, Bertrand, 132
Russians, 225

sacrifice, 126, 229
St. Paul, 253
St. Valentine's Day, 175, 185
San Francisco, 101
  -Palo Alto area, 135
Saturday Evening Post, The, 175
school problems, 83
Schopenhauer, 11, 22
security, 11, 34, 53, 58, 143
  bias towards, 62
  -conscious, 55
segregation, 67, 68
Seldon, John, 132
selection
  evolutionary, 75
  mate, 81
self-abuse, 65
selfishness, 67, 125-126
self-love, 153
sensitivity trainers, 200
sensuality, 105
sex
  act, 12, 206
  collective, 105
  "co-marital," 100
  extramarital, 52, 87-91, 230,
    248
  -for-support, 184
  legitimization, 238
  -marriage researcher, 48
  meaningful, 157
  monopoly, 206-207
  morals, 207
  object, 51, 53, 122, 176